THRIVING AFTER ADDICTION

THRIVING
After Addiction
A GUIDE TO HEAL, RECONNECT, AND *THRIVE* IN RECOVERY

ERIN GERAGHTY

MUTANT MANATEE PUBLISHING

THRIVING AFTER ADDICTION: A GUIDE TO HEAL, RECONNECT, AND *THRIVE* IN RECOVERY
Copyright © 2018 by Erin Geraghty

All rights reserved. No part of this book may be reproduced or utilized in any form or by any means, electronic or mechanical, including photocopying, recording, or by any information storage or retrieval system without permission in writing from the publisher.

This edition published 2018 by Mutant Manatee Publishing, Bradenton, Florida.

Colophon
Designed by Brendan Linzi using Adobe® InDesign.®
The typefaces used are Expo Serif Pro for the body text and chapter titles. Designed by Mark Jamra. From TypeCulture.

DISCLAIMER

The information provided in this book is designed to provide helpful information on the subjects discussed. This book is not meant to be used, nor should it be used, to diagnose or treat any medical condition. For diagnosis or treatment of any medical problem, consult your own physician. The publisher and author are not responsible for any specific health or allergy needs that may require medical supervision and are not liable for any damages or negative consequences from any treatment, action, application or preparation, to any person reading or following the information in this book. References are provided for informational purposes only and do not constitute endorsement of any websites or other sources. Readers should be aware that the websites listed in this book may change.

ACKNOWLEDGEMENTS

This book would not have been possible without the amazing people below.

To my editor Jamey Jones, I'm not sure I thanked you enough, so you are in my thank yous. You are truly skilled at what you do and I am so grateful we met each other in YTT and continued watching each other grow. Thank you for your patience, skill, and determination.

To Valeri Rose (Gigi RaMoan) my teammate and friend, who created the beautiful cover for this book, thank you so much. Every day I fall more in love with my heart fire girl.

To my coach mentor, Brooke Castillo, your work opened up my world. Thank you so much for all you produce for others. You have a gift and you're an inspiration.

Thank you Wendy for all you have given me coach wise, friend wise, and sister wise. You are a part of my heart.

Joe & Linda Matthews thank you so much for your generosity, your love, and belief in me from the very beginning. I love you both so much.

Don, it may have been just by chance you came into my life and the studio, but your kindness impacts thousands. Thank you.

To my father Lawrence P. Geraghty, you have been my life long life coach. Your integrity inspires me. In my darkest and brightest times, you were always there loving me as much as you could. Thank you.

To my mother, Deborah Ann Kosan, thank you for trusting in me to grow and evolve. I am who I am because of you.

To my best friend Mfon, Dude. It's been a hell of a ride. Even though we are on opposite sides of the country, we are evolving alongside each other in spirit. I love you so much.

To my friend T.O., Thank you for letting me be a part of your life and journey. I'm so excited for this next phase of your life. You mean the world to me.

To my soul brother Ian, even from across the globe coaching you was a miraculous experience. I will never forget it. Thank you for being in my realm.

Thank you Craig. This work was inspired mostly by your story. I know you were seeking a way out from all the pain. You left me my first copy of the Bhagavad Gita. Whether you knew it or not, it pointed towards the direction of my future. I found a way out, now I'm going to share it with everyone who is left from the gang.

To my Sensei Grandmaster James T. Martin Sr. I'm sorry you'll never get to read this sir, but I'll write it anyways. I learned how to funnel that tenacity you always saw in me and transmute it into something so beautiful. Thank you so much for tackling me that one day on the street and dragging me back. You made me fight and I love you so much for it.

To my mentor Frannie Hoffman, I never knew such softness and kindness existed until I met you. You continue to inspire me and I am so proud and honored to call you my friend. I love love love you.

To Joe and Linda Matthews, your generosity and belief in my has made this project possible. From letting me stay and write at both your homes, contributing to the kickstarter, and just being so encouraging, I feel blessed and incredibly grateful to have such wonderful supportive family. Thank you from the bottom of my heart.

To my loving husband Brendan. Absolutely none of this would be possible without you. Thank you for holding space for me to grow. Thank you for loving me before I knew how to love myself. Thank you for never giving up even when I pushed you away. I am so honored and excited to be on this journey of life with you.

x

Contents

Introduction	1
The Four Elements of Thriving After Addiction	7
Weeks One & Two—Taking Back Your Power	15
Weeks Three & Four: The Emotion Experience	33
Weeks Five & Six: Self-Love	51
Weeks Seven & Eight: Self-Care	69
Weeks Nine & Ten: Passion and Boundaries	85
Weeks Eleven & Twelve: Showing Up for Life	101
Conclusion	117
About the Author	121

INTRODUCTION

Every time I do it, I promise myself it's the last time. I flush the toilet and move on. This time it was a particularly violent purge because I didn't begin my binge with the usual ice cream, which helps everything come up easier. This time I didn't have the control to start with ice cream. I paid for it. But that didn't stop me from doing it again. I was purging around four times a day at this point, my last year of high school. And I kept that pace up for four more years.

The first time I made myself throw up to lose weight I was 16. My boyfriend at the time was an artist. He drew pictures of emaciated cartoon women with big breasts and a tiny waist. They looked nothing like me.

He and I were in the bathtub together one day when he told me, casually, "I don't love you anymore." It hit me like a truck. *It must be my body*, I thought. And so began my affair with bulimia.

It was my secret. I would pull up to a gas station, grab a pint of ice cream, candy bars, pastries, nuts—anything but chips; they hurt too much coming back up. I would eat it all before karate practice and then weigh myself. The number staring back at me from the scale stirred my self-hatred. That number was all the motivation I needed to purge. Afterward, a euphoric numbness washed over me when that number went down. That number was my validation. My control. When I had nothing, that number loved me back. Until I reached it.

THRIVING AFTER ADDICTION

That magic number was always an illusion. Chasing it thrilled me, but I was so obsessed with not accepting myself that every time I lost the weight, I felt shame that my ideal was still out of reach. I remember my goal was 145, and when I got to 143, I changed my goal to 135. I was searching for the feeling I thought that number would bring, but it never came.

I remember routinely scanning my body, mentally changing my thighs, my stomach, and my hips. If I rejected my body strongly enough, I thought it would change. I was sure of it. I decided that my body was not trustworthy. It was a beast I had to tame.

Sometimes, when I was close to my goal weight, I would see if I could purge just one more time to get there. One time I broke so many blood vessels in my left eye from all the pressure of trying to lose one more pound of weight. My eye was bloodshot for a week. I played it off like someone had cocked me in the face at karate. It fit right in with my story. I was tough.

***

I remember looking into my mother's eyes when I was a little girl. They were so blue and beautiful—so much prettier than mine. I adored her face, her smell, her touch. Sometimes she would stroke my hair. She would whisper to me, just a sound, and I melted. I didn't want it to end.

As I got older I noticed my mom had ups and downs. Some days she would lock herself in her room. I soon realized that when she was feeling down it was no longer safe for me to open up emotionally—to melt again as she pet my hair. I wanted her affection so badly. I started to copy her actions hoping she would

INTRODUCTION

notice.

My mother was always on a diet or using diet pills. When she was thin she was happy. She had energy. She loved me when she was thin. Then, slowly, as she became unhappy with her body again, she would become unavailable and her affections toward me lessened. She shut down. There were fewer hugs, and more yelling. I felt lost, and I blamed myself.

I first took my mother's diet pills when I was 15. I lost a lot of weight. That cloud of numb ecstasy, which I would later crave from my binges and purges, washed over me. All the pain of rejection faded. I felt powerful. I didn't want to curl up in a ball and disappear like usual. I was confident and funny and lovable. I got many compliments and attention from men. It didn't matter anymore if my mother loved me or not. I thought I didn't need her.

I didn't realize how much I had become her.

**

If you are reading this book, addiction has likely haunted your life. You know how to "not drink" or "not binge" or "not use" or "not gamble" or "not sleep with just anyone," but somehow, it's not enough to just quit. You know in your bones that something is missing. You long for it. You see others who have overcome addiction and are thriving. You also want to thrive. You have tasted excitement for life but struggle to find it on a daily basis.

Please know that the deeper connection to life you have been longing for is yours to have.

If you are still drinking, using, binging, or engaging with your addiction, this book is not enough to help you. I urge you to seek

THRIVING AFTER ADDICTION

help via a detox facility and/or support program. This book is for people already in recovery. Set it aside until you're ready.

I don't believe that addiction is a permanent disease or that it defines us. I believe it can be cured. I think it's a symptom of a deeper problem that is only discovered with a lot of work. Your addiction may even be the greatest gift you've been given. It can show you the work you need to do to become the person you are meant to be.

I was once told that the mind is the most powerful tool on the planet, but I humbly disagree. The body matches the mind in its intelligence. Have you ever had a gut feeling that went against everything you knew to be logical, and yet following your gut was the right decision, despite what your mind told you?

> **The connection of the mind and body is a sacred, profound experience that cultivates a wisdom in us that can't be found elsewhere.**

The connection of the mind and body is a sacred, profound experience that cultivates a wisdom in us that can't be found elsewhere. When the mind and body are disconnected, we feel incomplete, searching for answers, solutions, satisfaction, security, compassion, and love outside of ourselves where we'll never find it.

Eckhart Tolle would say that searching is the antithesis of being. He would say we act like *humans searching* rather than *human beings*. This familiar pattern begins when we are young as we form attachments to people, food, places, toys, etc. We begin to attribute our sense of peace to these outside things. We think, "(blank) makes me feel better." Our feelings become wrapped up

INTRODUCTION

with the objects we encounter.

Our brain and body pick up on this relationship and a neural pathway of recognition is formed. In yoga, we call these pathways *samskaras*. They are like grooves in the mind that connect a desire with a sensory, emotional, or intellectual experience that either pleases or displeases us. These samskaras condition us to spend an enormous amount of time seeking pleasure and avoiding discomfort. When taken to the extreme, this search for pleasure can result in addiction. Understanding and recognizing these patterns within ourselves is an important part of breaking free from the hold they have on us.

By removing the addictive substance of choice from your life, you have removed its grip from your psyche. But it's likely that you are filling the remaining holes with behaviors or thoughts that are keeping you from living the life you have always longed for.

I wrote this book to help you understand that what you have always been searching for cannot be found in a substance or activity. The work of the Thriving After Addiction program involves rewriting your mental, emotional, and physical patterns—your samskaras—in a way that helps you to feel that you have finally found what you've always been searching for. I created this program, integrating the physical, mental, emotional, and spiritual parts of you that have lost each other. Your search is over. You can stop filling the holes in your life with destructive patterns.

This book will help you shed sabotaging beliefs so you can repair your relationship with yourself and others, and show up in the world with passion and drive.

Thriving after addiction occurs when you nourish your body, still your mind, understand your circumstances, and connect to

THRIVING AFTER ADDICTION

your true self. This book will show you how. It's a 12-week program broken into two-week increments, each two weeks building on the last two. By the end of the program, you will have created new habits and patterns in your mind and body that create a new perspective and new way of being that you can carry with you for the rest of your life.

CHAPTER ONE

THE FOUR ELEMENTS OF THRIVING AFTER ADDICTION

Most addicts in recovery live in an intermediate state that feels just outside of where they want to be. They no longer rely on their addictive substance or behavior, which they think should help them feel as though life is fulfilling, but something is still missing.

I felt this way after I quit drinking, taking pills, and binging and purging. I should have been on cloud nine, but I wasn't. *This is it?* I thought. *Shouldn't I be on top of the world right now?* It's what drives some addicts back into addiction.

I felt emotional. Strong feelings would wash over me and I didn't know what to do with them. I had always numbed these feelings with food or booze or pills. Now I had nowhere to hide from them. It was overwhelming at times. I wondered if something was wrong with me.

It wasn't until I found yoga and began meditating that I could feel safe with my own emotions. Further exploration via life coaching helped me to understand and transform these emotions. And when I implemented a sound nutritional program, my body, mind, emotions, and spirit finally felt aligned. It was like coming home.

That's why I created the Thriving After Addiction program. It worked phenomenally for me, and so I began to use it with my addiction clients. When I witnessed the effects it had on the lives of people who had struggled with varying addictions, I knew I had to share it with more people.

THRIVING AFTER ADDICTION

The program requires full dedication for at least 12 weeks. Ideally, you will incorporate the elements of the program into your life so that it becomes a way of living rather than a temporary fix. Twelve weeks can change your life, and it can only get better from there. After fully participating in the program you will feel a sense of ease and lightness, and be filled with more love and motivation than you have felt in a long time. Why stop after 12 weeks?

> Your addiction was a gift that will teach you to dig deeper.

The Thriving After Addiction program is made up of four parts working simultaneously. They build upon and complement each other. They are the ingredients of the secret recipe to your freedom.

Your addiction was a gift that will teach you to dig deeper. Here's a shovel.

NUTRITION

Addiction takes its toll on the body. I abused my body so badly that my hormones became unbalanced and I was probably a few bad decisions away from developing a chronic disease. My nervous system was fried. I was constantly achy and fatigued. Maybe you feel similarly.

I include a nutrition component to my program because I find it sorely missing from other addiction recovery programs. In order for us to fully heal, our bodies must come along for the ride. The nutrition recommendations I make in this program are basic yet important steps toward rebuilding your health.

Your body is your temple—it houses your soul. Caring for your

THE FOUR ELEMENTS OF THRIVING AFTER ADDICTION

temple will help you to cultivate a strong, respectful relationship with yourself so that you can move, breathe, act, and feel empowered like never before.

Each two-week period you will incorporate a new nutritional habit so that by the end of the program, you will have established a strong foundation of health. You will likely experience digestive benefits, increased energy, and even emotional and mental improvements from the changes you make.

> Caring for your temple will help you to cultivate a strong, respectful relationship with yourself so that you can move, breathe, act, and feel empowered like never before.

YOGA—ASANA AND PHILOSOPHY

Yoga is an ancient science that teaches us how to connect the mind and body through a series of postures, ethics, observances, breath control, meditation, and surrender. In the West, we tend to view yoga as only the physical postures, also called *asana*. But asana is only the tip of the iceberg. Underneath the physical practice is what my clients have called the "glue" of the Thriving After Addiction program—the yoga helps hold it all together. I agree.

You may think of yoga in the same way I did the first time I experienced a yoga class: "fucking stupid." Sometimes yoga moves slow and invites us to "open our hearts" or "just let go" or any number of woo-woo phrases that might seem meaningless. Withhold your judgement. Give the practice some time. Trust me when I say that it works in mysterious ways. It requires a bit of surrender.

THRIVING AFTER ADDICTION

Yoga teaches us the depths of ourselves, but it begins as a simple practice. You will start with a short asana practice that you will build upon as the program unfolds. Yoga is usually perceived as a stretching exercise that can help relieve stress and help to manage or relieve pain. While this is all true, yoga goes much deeper than that. As a yoga therapist, I have seen new people emerge in as little as four weeks of practice three times per week. The magic of yoga is that, with regular practice, you will get out of it what you seek from it, and usually so much more.

There is something about yoga that can access places within you that no amount of thinking, feeling, or exercising can. Working with addiction clients, I have witnessed the power of yoga to help people recover and heal from physical, emotional, and mental stress. I have learned that, for some people, no amount of life coaching will work until the body is ready to experience emotions. Yoga paves the way for this experience. Rough edges and defenses simply melt away with every twist, forward fold, and passive back bend.

Yoga is the glue of my program. Over the course of twelve weeks, you will build your yoga practice from a few-minute warm up to a full sixty-minute practice that you can do anywhere. Please don't skip the practices. They are integral to your healing. Practice the postures *at least* three times weekly—daily if possible. The practices gradually get longer as the weeks go on so that you can ease into the practice gradually.

I have taught yoga to everyone from the perfectly poised athlete to the woman with reconstructive shoulder surgery. I have worked with people who could not get up from or down to the ground without help, with people undergoing chemotherapy and

THE FOUR ELEMENTS OF THRIVING AFTER ADDICTION

radiation treatments, and with clients experiencing paralysis from spinal cord injuries. I have taught yoga to people ages four to 94. If you are unsure about your ability to practice, don't be. Talk to your doctor about engaging in a yoga practice. If you have certain restrictions, you can follow the Chair Yoga practice video, available on thrivingafteraddiction.com/thriving-after-addiction-book-program, to get the benefits of the practice.

In addition to the yoga asana, you will learn yoga philosophies that will help to cement the concepts of each chapter into your mind and way of life. The yoga philosophies I share with you touch on some basic ethics and practices that will guide you to live a life aligned with your true self. These philosophies are the yoga you will take off your mat and into your life. The physical asana practice simply helps prepare the body to better understand and integrate the yoga philosophy. The two go hand in hand.

LIFE COACHING

The life coaching component of the Thriving After Addiction program is what really makes the program unique. Life coaching is a method of inquiry and self-study that allows you to rid yourself of painful thoughts and beliefs, and regain clarity and direction in your life. With practice, you will learn to identify thoughts as separate from your true nature so that you can observe them objectively. In this light, you will be able to choose, with compassion, whether your thoughts serve you or whether you don't need

> As the creator of your thoughts, you will take full accountability of their outcomes.

them anymore. As the creator of your thoughts, you will take full accountability of their outcomes. Then you will use tools to change the thoughts that no longer serve you.

Many people use a life coach to help them create space between themselves and their thoughts, but it is possible to do this work on your own. This program will walk you through some foundational life coaching work.

MEDITATION

Meditation changes your brain, literally. Studies have found that a regular meditation practice helps preserve brain aging; reduces brain activity in the brain's default mode network, the brain network responsible for a wandering mind; rivals antidepressants for depression and anxiety; improves concentration and attention; reduces social anxiety; and can help with addiction.

One eight-week meditation study by Harvard researchers found that a regular meditation practice—either a mindfulness meditation or a compassion meditation—has beneficial effects on emotional processing, even long after the meditation session is over. You will learn both types of meditation in the Thriving After Addiction program, along with others.

"Prayer is when you speak to God; Meditation is when you listen to God."

—*Anonymous*

Many meditation studies suggest that as little as ten to 12 minutes of daily meditation produces beneficial effects. The Thriving

THE FOUR ELEMENTS OF THRIVING AFTER ADDICTION

After Addiction program will introduce you to a few different meditations styles so that you can find a method that you will stick with. You will set aside a few minutes each day for meditation practice, building week-by-week. Some days you will feel as though it's impossible to "follow along" with the meditation. Some days it will feel easy. That's normal. Try to withhold judgement about the quality of your meditation. There is no "good" or "bad" meditation. There is just meditation.

Meditation is introduced right from the start of the Thriving After Addiction program because it helps you create space in your mind, slowing down the incessant mind-chatter that gets in the way of clarity and insight. Imagine trying to write down your thoughts as some asshole keeps pointing his leaf blower at you. Your papers fly everywhere, you get frustrated, and you lose your focus. Your overactive mind is that asshole blowing tons of thoughts your way. Meditation turns off the leaf blower so that you can focus more easily, feel calmer, and reconnect to your true self.

If the idea of sitting cross-legged on the floor with your eyes closed for an hour sounds like the *last* thing you want to do, you're not alone. A meditation practice is one of the most accessible practices you can add to your daily routine, but it doesn't seem that way from the outside. If sitting cross legged on a cushion or the floor is not comfortable for you, sitting in a chair is a great alternative. Comfort is key.

To enhance your meditation experience, I have created audio meditations for every two-week period of the Thriving After Addiction program that you can download and listen to daily to help guide your meditation. Visit thrivingafteraddiction.com/

THRIVING AFTER ADDICTION

thriving-after-addiction-book-program to listen to them or download as you go.

WEEKS ONE & TWO—TAKING BACK YOUR POWER

CHAPTER TWO

WEEKS ONE & TWO—TAKING BACK YOUR POWER

"How do you react when you think you need people's love? Do you become a slave for their approval? Do you live an inauthentic life because you can't bear the thought that they might disapprove of you? Do you try to figure out how they would like you to be, and then try to become that, like a chameleon? In fact, you never really get their love. You turn into someone you aren't, and when they say, "I love you," you can't believe it because you are loving a façade. They're loving someone who doesn't even exist."

—Byron Katie, <u>Question Your Thinking, Change the World</u>

My oldest brother was addicted to crack, but he would use other drugs and alcohol when he couldn't get it. His favorite names for me were slut and whore. He broke my nose one day when I was 13. I had yelled at him for beating the shit out of his pit bull, so he attacked me. My mother eventually kicked him out of the house. He nearly tore my family apart.

That same year I began karate. It was a natural progression for me. It gave me a great work ethic, a physical outlet, and a sensei, my teacher, who I could look up to and who was there for me. I spent eight years of my life sweating, kicking, being tossed around, winning state championships, and following a discipline. In karate, kicking and punching people was encouraged. It was the perfect outlet for the violence inside me. I could work until my body hurt. It was okay to punish myself. And others.

My sensei, Master James T. Martin Sr., was tough as nails. He was just what I needed—extremely strict. He gave me names like Brick Shithouse, Buffalo Chubbs and with an encouraging smile, reminded me how much better I would perform if I lost about 15lbs. The names hurt but also felt oddly satisfying. It felt true that I could never be fully accepted and loved. I was just happy to be noticed. He showed up for me when many others didn't.

By 16, I had earned my brown belt. One night after some intense sparring, I felt beaten down. My emotions got the best of me, but he kept pushing. My sensei was old school and taught me to keep my hands up by repeatedly popping me in the face. After one particular jab, I started to cry. I tore off my brown belt and threw it to the floor.

"I don't need this dojo," I erupted like a fiery volcano, "And I don't need you."

His eyes were furious and I felt the fear of God in my heart. I did what anyone with survival instincts would do—I fucking booked.

I fell down half a flight of stairs while putting on my shoes and shoving my gear into my bag. "Red, get back here," he yelled.

I ran as fast as I possibly could. About half a block from the dojo, sensei roared up behind me like The Terminator and put me in the most gripping and secure headlock I've ever experienced.

Forgetting he was a grandmaster for a moment, I flailed my arms trying to hit him. He could snap my neck like a twig if he wanted to. In a raspy yet soothing voice he said, "Red, you gotta come back to the dojo. The girls need you. You're strong. It's your home."

I cried.

I had a home. They needed me. Despite one final urge to flee, the pull of a family I had always longed for was too strong. I

WEEKS ONE & TWO—TAKING BACK YOUR POWER

surrendered.

"I'll let you go now if you promise not to run away," sensei said, still holding me.

"Yes sir," I said, completely deflated.

Back at the dojo he put me in my fighting stance and pointed to the old, tattered poster on the wall, which read, "Winners Never Quit, Quitters Never Win."

"We don't quit here," he said. "Now go fight."

I spent the next five years fighting.

***

A year later I was sitting in the back seat of my friend Sam's car. He took out a vial and wrapped his bicep tight with a rubber band. He flicked the vial a few times. "Air in the blood will kill you," he said.

"I thought you had stopped," I said, wide-eyed.

He looked at me with that charming smile, "I am, but I wanted to do it one last time with my brother." *One last time*, I thought. I was curious but never curious enough to join them.

***

It's time to dig. Grab a shovel.

As an addict in recovery, you have already taken massive action to create change in your life when the suffering became too great. It is absolutely the fight of your life. It can feel like the weight of the world is crushing you, but you still grasp onto something within you that keeps you going. By the time you are fully in recovery, you are exhausted. Sure, you have won the battle with your addiction, but it doesn't feel like the fight is over. You still feel somewhat defeated even though you think you should feel on top of the world because you quit your addiction.

The thing is, if you haven't traced your addiction down to its root and plucked it out from its deepest tip, you will still struggle with an addictive mind and may latch onto a new habit that continues to drain your life force and prevent you from becoming who you are meant to be.

Even if most of your moments feel content and fueled with passion, you likely still succumb to days when you feel as though you have an itch that can't be scratched. You're still searching, but you're not sure what for. There is more work to be done.

For the next two weeks, you will incorporate nutrition, yoga, and meditation habits that will help you establish a solid foundation, all while practicing self-led life coaching techniques designed to help you better understand and modify the tendencies of your mind. After two weeks, you will be ready to do the deeper work that comes with understanding and connecting with your emotions.

NUTRITION

This week you will increase your water intake. Most people don't drink nearly enough water, if they drink any at all. Your body is made up of 80 percent water. Replenishing this vital liquid is crucial for the function of every cell in your body. Beginning today you will drink three liters of spring water every day. Carry a water bottle with you to keep track of your water intake. Drink

WEEKS ONE & TWO—TAKING BACK YOUR POWER

the water throughout the day rather than all at once.

Next, you will add one to two teaspoons of Celtic sea salt to your food. Sea salt is full of minerals such as magnesium, calcium, potassium, iron, zinc, and iodine—all essential to health. Replace your table salt with Celtic salt. If you eat a diet high in processed foods, begin to eliminate these foods from your diet. Instead, prepare foods at home, adding Celtic sea salt to replace poor quality salt from processed foods.

YOGA ASANA

This week, you will learn Sun Salutations. This practice will take just five minutes, but can be considered a full yoga practice. The movements are designed to help you link your breath with movement and take your body through a range of motion that warms you up, preparing you for your day. Sun Salutations are best practiced in the morning, but if that doesn't work for your schedule, you can do them any time.

Visit thrivingafteraddiction.com/thriving-after-addiction-book-program to view the yoga video for weeks one & two to follow along with the practice. All you will need is a yoga mat and enough space to feel comfortable moving on the mat. Wear comfortable clothing and remove your socks to get good traction on your mat.

THRIVING AFTER ADDICTION

YOGA PHILOSOPHY

Ahimsa and Satya

Ahimsa is the yogic principle of nonviolence toward all living things. With addiction, ahimsa toward yourself and others can stop the cycles of pain you have created in your life. In particular, the more you treat *yourself* with respect and compassion, the more you will notice the world around you shift. Nonviolence toward yourself will prepare you for the life coaching work you do during the next two weeks. As you begin to understand your anger, sadness, and frustration, remaining compassionate toward yourself is crucial.

Satya is the yogic principle of truthfulness. The work you do this week will require you to be completely honest with yourself. Not only do we sometimes lie to others, we often lie to ourselves. Recognize when you are being harsh on yourself. Take rest when you need it. As you become familiar with your inner dialogue, some truths will emerge. If these truths send a shockwave through your body, you'll know that's where your work will need to focus.

As you become nonviolent and truthful with yourself, you will begin to emerge feeling safe, excited, joyful, and passionate. And in the words of Marianne Williamson, spiritual activist, author, lecturer, and founder of The Peace Alliance:

> *As we let our own light shine, we unconsciously give other people permission to do the same.*
>
> —Maryanne Williamson

WEEKS ONE & TWO—TAKING BACK YOUR POWER

LIFE COACHING

I need to start off by introducing you to a simple yet profound concept that comes from many different philosophies. To gain a better understanding of your thoughts and patterns—and to take back your power—you will need to break down any situation you encounter into its components:

- Circumstances

- (Look at Your) Thoughts

- Emotions

- Actions

- Results

If you ever forget the formula, just remember the acronym: CLEAR. By separating every element, our mind becomes more clear and we are able to work through whatever obstacle we are stuck on. Below I break the formula down further.

Circumstances are the facts. To reduce the drama you create around any situation, it's helpful to tease out the simple facts from what your mind. Your mind will create an entire story worthy of CNN coverage about even the least significant of circumstances. Finding the hard facts in any situation will be like sifting for gold—full of value.

Circumstances are those occurrences that we take in from our senses—what we see, hear, feel, taste, or smell.

Here is an example from my own life:

> When we don't supervise our thoughts, we end up relinquishing control and feeling like a victim.

My mother brought up a comment my ex-husband had once said about me just to embarrass me at dinner with my new boyfriend. It felt like a circumstance, but let's take a closer look.

Circumstance: My mother brought up a comment my ex-husband had once said about me during dinner with my new boyfriend.

Thought: She did that on purpose! She's trying to sabotage my new relationship so I can be as miserable as she is.

You can see how my mind ran away with this one. But when we break it down, it's easy to see that facts are neutral. It's the judgement we create about the fact that becomes upsetting. Look how much power I handed over! I gave my mother complete control over my relationship. When we don't supervise our thoughts, we end up relinquishing control and feeling like a victim.

Thoughts as in "Look at your Thoughts." Thoughts are opinions or judgments we create in our minds in response to the facts in our lives. To keep it simple, a thought could be, "That tastes amazing," or "I don't like how that feels." Our thoughts are usually based on our past conditioning and experiences. As adults, we always have the ability to choose our thoughts, but because we choose particular thoughts over and over in response to certain circumstances, we form belief systems that can be difficult to separate from.

Reality is what we make of it, literally. It can help to take a

WEEKS ONE & TWO — TAKING BACK YOUR POWER

step back from our belief systems, which are just well-practiced thoughts, in order to understand what is really true.

Emotions. Thoughts are essentially electromagnetic energy that catalyzes vibrations in the form of emotions. When I thought about my mother trying to sabotage my relationship, a wave of anger washed over me. Thoughts trigger emotions, and they often create a vicious cycle. When I became angry about my mother's comment, it reminded me of how I was trying desperately to not be like her despite years of doing just the opposite. That fueled my anger and reminded me of my shame. Thoughts and emotions are intricately entwined and are a dangerous combination that can quickly escalate a simple comment into a full-blown feud.

Actions. Once we get carried away with our emotions, we act upon them. This is when trouble can begin. When we are wrapped up in a negative emotion, even if we are trying to suppress it in the moment, our actions are affected. Sometimes we lash out at others. Sometimes we punish ourselves. Sometimes we swallow our emotions and withdraw, eventually acting on them later.

When my anger at my mother overcame me, I withdrew by putting up an emotional barrier. I stewed quietly until I got home, at which point I binged on food because I felt that the anger was out of my control. Then I resented my mother for causing me to binge.

Results. With every action, there is a reaction. Everything we do in life has a consequence, some good and some not so good. When I was angry with my mother and withdrew from her, I felt justified in hurting her feelings. I felt resentful and disconnected, and this affected our relationship as well as my relationship to myself. These were the results from my actions.

THRIVING AFTER ADDICTION

For the next two weeks, every time you have a strong emotional response to a situation, take some time to later deconstruct what happened. Start with the facts. Then identify the thoughts that arose. Recognize what emotions followed and whether the thought-emotion cycle pulled in more thoughts and yet more emotions. Then think about the consequences of it all. Take a few minutes every day to journal about these components. It will feel tedious at first, but practicing with effort on a regular basis will yield great results. For more guidance about how to do this work, tune into my podcast ***Thriving After Addiction***, episode 8, *Boundaries for Healthy Relationships*.

- Circumstances
- (Look at Your) Thoughts
- Emotions
- Actions
- Results

The more comfortable you get at recognizing this sequence of events, the more mindful you will become when caught in a moment that unravels. Over time, you will begin to see that those thoughts that arise in response to neutral facts no longer have such a hold over you. It will be as though you have taken a step back to witness the events of your life as neutral circumstances that have much less an effect on you than they used to.

WEEKS ONE & TWO—TAKING BACK YOUR POWER

While it sounds simple, this process takes practice. Your daily meditation will aid you by helping you become more aware of your circumstances moment by moment. Trust the process as it unfolds. You can also do stream of consciousness journaling to help you better understand your thought processes. Without filtering or editing, write down everything that comes to mind. Taking five to ten minutes a day to do this can give you some real insight about your thought patterns, the emotions that arise from those thoughts, and the actions and consequences that follow.

In my own example, when my mother brought up my ex-husband's comment, if I had instead asked my mother in the moment if we could change the subject, or if could have recognized that my mother's comment had nothing to do with me but was only a reflection of her own view of the world, I would not have experienced such emotional pain or suffered the consequences.

Claim Your Power

When I walked into my spiritual teacher Frannie Hoffman's office for the first time, she asked me right away about my relationship with my parents. "Specifically, your mother," she said.

I gulped. My mother was my trigger for binging, numbing out with pills, and rebelling with alcohol. So many of my negative behaviors stemmed from my desire for her attention. What I was really doing was giving her my power. I relinquished my control to her. She didn't ask for it, but I willingly gave up my power to her.

I have given up my power to my mentors too, especially my karate sensei. Maybe you have also done this. Have you ever felt as though you had to sacrifice yourself for someone else in order to be accepted by them? Why do we *do* that?

It stems from childhood. The way we attach to our parents

plays a big role in how we play out relationships throughout our life. Some of us end up feeling like we don't matter, and some of us end up feeling like we're not enough. Sometimes, we feel both, especially if we have experienced trauma.

Deep down, we all want acceptance and love from our parents or caregivers, but our minds distort how we go about getting it. We hide underneath behaviors and emotions that mask our basic truths, and when we don't feel like we matter, or that we are enough, we become disappointed. This is one of the most common issues I coach my clients on.

If you want someone's love but you are constantly pretending to be someone you aren't, of course you are going to be riddled with self-doubt. If you bury your true self for too long you begin to forget who you really are. You get so good at being the person you think others want you to be that you lose your true self.

> **Blame only places your power in someone else's hands.**

Consider how you act when your parents don't accept you. Some people try to make up for it by becoming a people-pleaser, going out of their way to do anything and everything they can to win back that love. And some people rebel and shut their parents out. Sometimes people take on the negative attributes of one parent only to antagonize the other parent. Either way, we sacrifice our authenticity and later wonder why we feel so lost in life. Most of my clients have no idea this is brewing under the surface until we explore the dynamic in depth.

To correct your misperceptions, you have to take back your power. First, you must acknowledge that your parents have no control over your feelings. Your life has unfolded exactly as it

WEEKS ONE & TWO—TAKING BACK YOUR POWER

needed to, given the circumstances, in order for you to grow. Blame will get you nowhere. Blame only places your power in someone else's hands.

The questions below will walk you through pain and blame so that you can come out the other side claiming your power. It is meant to feel cathartic. Take your time with these questions.

Who is the person(s) you believe has caused you the most pain in your life (past or present)?
_____

Think of an exact situation that angered, saddened, scared, or disappointed you, and describe it in detail.
_____
_____

Now, list only the circumstances (facts) about that situation. (Remember, no opinions or judgements. Only include facts.)
_____
_____

Now, what do those facts mean to you? (What are your opinions and judgments about what happened?)
_____
_____

How does the situation make you feel?
_____
_____

THRIVING AFTER ADDICTION

When you feel that way, how do you act?
_____
_____

What are the results of your actions?
_____

Imagine who you would be if you knew that your thoughts about this situation were incorrect. How would things change? How would you feel? How would you act differently?
_____
_____

Pain Points

Now that you know how to distinguish between facts, which are neutral, and the thoughts, emotions, actions, and consequences that you pile onto the facts of your life, you are better equipped to examine your big pain points. I told you to grab your shovel—it's time to dig. You will start digging at your pain points.

Pain points are those areas of life that cause you the most emotional pain. Before you correct me by saying that emotional pain comes from our own minds and not our circumstances (you have been paying attention!), I'll rephrase: pain points are those areas of life where you attribute the negative thoughts (and thus emotions, actions, and consequences) to the neutral circumstances (facts) of your life. What do you struggle with most? Certain relationships may trigger your emotional pain. Or it might be your career. Or maybe your emotional pain comes from your

WEEKS ONE & TWO—TAKING BACK YOUR POWER

body and appearance, like mine.

The disgust I have felt about my body has been the cause of most of my emotional pain. I remember waking up almost every day and staring in the mirror at all the parts of my body I hated. As I scanned myself I imagined how amazing my life would be if I lost weight in all the right places. I developed unhealthy habits to achieve that weight loss. When I finally lost the weight and achieved that so-called amazing life, I was more miserable than ever.

I finally realized that my emotional pain didn't come from my body after all. My body is like a neutral fact—it is what it is. The thoughts that arose about my body—and the ensuing emotions, actions, and consequences—are what truly caused all my emotional pain. Once I realized this, I began digging for the statement replaying in my mind that triggered my pain.

It came back to a lack of one of the two main attachment needs: I am not enough.

Usually, it sounded like this in my head: "What's wrong with you Erin?" Sometimes, it came from other people. Something was always wrong with me. I was never enough, as is. Something needed to change for me to be the person I always wanted to be, at least in my head.

To discover your pain points, it will help to answer the following questions in letter format. Who or what seems to be the biggest cause of pain in your life? If there are more than one, then write a letter to each one. Your pain point may be someone else. It may be yourself. It may be a situation in your life. Lay all your thoughts and emotions out in the letter.

THRIVING AFTER ADDICTION

Dear _____,

I am angry with/about you because _____
_____.

It makes me feel sad because _____
_____.

I wish _____
_____.

I just want to feel: like I matter / that I am enough. (Choose one.)

I am sorry about _____
_____.

I love you because _____
_____.

If you have trouble addressing the last statement, you can leave it blank for now. But come back to it at the end of the program. You will likely be ready to open to this emotion by then.

For me, the first pain point that helped me experience an incredible release was my relationship with my karate sensei. I loved him despite the way he treated me, and it caused me a lot of shame. It has been one of the most painful realizations of my life. I gave him so much power because I was desperate for love.

When I explored this pain point, which had been plaguing me for years, I was left feeling so peaceful and light. I finally developed

WEEKS ONE & TWO—TAKING BACK YOUR POWER

the ability to be proud of myself. I had taken my power back. I had an amazing shift in energy. Instead of feeling like something was wrong with me, or like I wasn't enough, I realized that I am amazing. I am enough, exactly as I am.

Digging down to your underlying needs is key to changing how you feel about yourself and your circumstances. Until you fully accept your basic need, you will be unable to change the negative thoughts, emotions, actions, and consequences that arise in response to the circumstances of your life.

You matter, and you are enough, just as you are. I know this to be absolutely true. Do you?

MEDITATION

Now that you have done the work around your pain points and discovered your basic needs, the meditation for this week is simple. Find a comfortable seated position, either on the floor, on a cushion, or in a chair. Sit with your back erect, lengthening your spine and relaxing your shoulders. You can place your hands together in your lap or separate on your thighs.

Set a timer for five minutes. Begin to take slow, deep breaths in and out through the nose. Let your breath be soft. Every time you exhale say your basic need in your head: "I am enough" or "I matter."

You will find that your mind begins to wander. You will begin to think about other people, situations, conversations, food, an itch on your head—all sorts of thoughts will come to your mind. Every time you find that your mind has wandered away from your breath and your basic need, bring your attention back and repeat your basic need as you exhale again. It's okay if you feel distracted. It happens. Stay with it and continue to redirect your attention for the entire five minutes.

Try to do this practice every day. You can find five minutes, I know it.

If you would like to follow along with a guided meditation, visit thrivingafteraddiction.com/thriving-after-addiction-book-program and follow weeks 1 & 2 for a yoga practice, meditation, and life coaching video to further guide you.

CHAPTER THREE

WEEKS THREE & FOUR: THE EMOTION EXPERIENCE

The function of mindfulness is, first, to recognize the suffering and then to take care of the suffering. The work of mindfulness is first to recognize the suffering and second, to embrace it...

So the practice is not to fight or suppress the feeling, but rather to cradle it with a lot of tenderness. When a mother embraces her child, that energy of tenderness begins to penetrate into the body of the child. If we can recognize and cradle the suffering while we breathe mindfully, there is relief already.

—Thich Nhat Hanh, <u>No Mud, No Lotus: The Art of Transforming Suffering</u>

At fifteen, I was hanging out with an older crowd. The thrill of getting into a college party juxtaposed with my anxiety and unworthiness kept me in a vulnerable, awkward state at these events. At one party, we quickly warmed up to the guy and girl who lived there. Their house became our new hang out. The guy was a D.J. and the girl spun fire. We thought they were cool as hell.

One weekend we were partying at their house when another friend spiked our drinks with so much LSD that even a hardcore hallucinogenic connoisseur would cower—all without our knowing. "You guys just took the most acid I've ever seen!" he laughed.

My heart skipped a beat. One friend took out a Sharpie pen and furiously wrote on his chest "I love you Mom" followed by his phone number. He said if someone found his dead body he wanted his mom to know.

THRIVING AFTER ADDICTION

We all went insane for 24 hours. Fucking insane. I became convinced that no one could stand me and I'd be kicked out of the group. I clung desperately to whoever was near. I remember drinking a wine cooler just to occupy myself before I blacked out into utter chaos. When I came to we were walking in the woods in a nearby park. At one point, the war in my mind came to life and I was projecting it everywhere. I saw darkness caving in on me as explosions roared around my body. I remember screaming and trembling as my heart beat nearly exploded out of my chest with fear. "Erin, chill the fuck out," my friends told me. The next thing I remember was running naked as fast as I could, past traffic, down the road, and all the way to the place I knew was safe—my house.

I threw myself against the glass door of our front porch. My mother opened the door shaking and screaming, thinking I had been raped. Maybe I had been. I wasn't sure.

***

At 16 I drove drunk and crashed my car into a pole. The DUI was a harsh wake up call. My drinking had gotten out of control. My need to fit in was ruining my life. But my ego loved to be known as the invincible badass. On the days when I bothered to show up to class, I would often get into fights—with girls, guys, it didn't matter. I wanted to inflict the pain I felt inside on anyone I could. One day I snapped a guy's collarbone for taunting me when I was drunk. I was good at hurting people.

While shopping at the mall one day, the girl making my sandwich at the food court recognized me. When I couldn't recall how

WEEKS THREE & FOUR: THE EMOTION EXPERIENCE

I knew her, she politely reminded me that I had punched her in the face repeatedly until her face was bloody and raw one night at a punk rock show. She showed me the scar on her head where I had bashed her head into the sidewalk. I just blinked at her. I felt like such a worthless asshole as I watched her carefully make my sandwich.

People who knew me then look at me now, spreading peace and love at my yoga studio, like, "Really?" Yeah, really. I was a fucking monster filled with insatiable rage and endless pain.

***

The addicts in recovery I have coached each have a story about what drove them to their addiction. Molestation, abandonment, poverty, death of someone close, modeled drug use, and emotional and physical abuse are common triggers. No matter the circumstances—whether traumatic or mild—emotional pain is part of your story, although you may have been hiding from it. I competed in full-contact sports for the better part of my life because physical pain helped me numb the emotional pain I kept hidden inside. My food addiction and substance abuse did, too.

In many cases, your subconscious voice—the judgmental one that often degrades you—is a reflection of an emotionally abusive parent, spouse, or someone close to you. You may not even know it. That's been my experience with many clients. Such destructive thoughts become our beliefs because they are so familiar. These thoughts trigger emotional experiences in us that, as you've learned, can lead to negative actions and consequences. But the familiarity of the initial beliefs and the emotions that follow are so ingrained in us that it becomes difficult to break the pattern.

In fact, it is difficult to even *see* the pattern. But over the last two weeks you've been working on recognizing the thoughts, emotions, actions, and consequences in your life, and how they arise from your response to simple facts. Now that you know how to separate the circumstances in your life—the facts—from all the "stuff" you attach to them, it's time to cozy up to your emotions.

Many people have a hard time sitting with their emotions, especially negative ones. Sadness, shame, disappointment, jealousy—we push those down or run from them so we don't have to be uncomfortable. The one negative emotion we seem to be okay with is anger. But anger is almost always a cover for a deeper, more vulnerable emotion. We express anger because we feel as though it protects us from going to that deeper place where the true emotion hides.

The only way to change the way you feel is to actually *feel* it. You can't run from emotion. You can't suppress emotion. It will always resurface, again and again, until you learn how to actually feel it. That's our work for the next couple weeks.

To prepare for the emotional work, you will also nourish your body and mind. The nutrition and yoga components of this program are essential for keeping you grounded and healthy. The physical, mental, emotional, and spiritual aspects of the Thriving After Addiction program are symbiotic—they each support the others.

NUTRITION

Continue to drink three liters of water, and add one to two

WEEKS THREE & FOUR: THE EMOTION EXPERIENCE

teaspoons of Celtic salt to your food every day, as you did in weeks one and two. Each week you add on a new nutritional practice that complements those of previous weeks. By the end of the program you will have developed nutritional habits that can support your throughout your life.

This week you will prepare a lemon drink that will support your immune and digestive health. Packed with fiber to help with regular bowel elimination; acid to help stimulate the flow of bile, which breaks down fats and carries toxins out of the body; and vitamin C to support adrenal and immune health, this drink is sure to have a beneficial impact.

Blend one whole lemon, cut in half—peel, seeds, and all—with a teaspoon of honey or a serving of stevia in a high-powered blender with eight ounces of water. Drink daily. I like to drink mine in the morning.

Once this drink becomes a regular part of your day, feel free to double the recipe and drink it twice daily. I do this and love it. This one drink has made a big impact on my own health and on the health of many of my clients.

Despite how it sounds, you will likely find that you enjoy this little drink more than you might think. Give it a try. Your body will thank you.

YOGA ASANA

This week, you will add on to your Sun Salutations. The practice will take ten minutes. The movements will continue to help you link your breath with movement, add some strength and coordination, and prepare your body and mind for a great day ahead.

Continue to practice at the same time of day you have been. It will help you create a habit that you can carry on.

If you would like to follow along with a guided meditation, visit <u>thrivingafteraddiction.com/thriving-after-addiction-book-program</u> and follow weeks 3 & 4 for a yoga practice, meditation, and life coaching video to further guide you.

YOGA PHILOSOPHY

Svadhyaya

Svadhyaya is the yogic principle of self-study. For the next two weeks, you will build on weeks one and two by continuing to be aware of your thought and emotion patterns so that you can sit with your emotions as they arise. Instead of explaining away your emotions, putting them aside, or ignoring them, you will take time to feel them as they come. Have you heard the saying, "The only way out is through"? To shed your negative thought and emotion patterns, you must be present for them. Learning how to do that—the purpose of this book—is svadhyaya. You are now fully immersed in your own self-study. The possibilities are endless.

Asteya

Asteya is the yogic principle of non-stealing. Asteya is often rooted in the false beliefs that you are not enough, you do not have enough, or you do not do enough. In response to these beliefs, you seek that which does not belong to you. It's the

WEEKS THREE & FOUR: THE EMOTION EXPERIENCE

grass-is-greener syndrome. You want for what you do not have. The result? Emotional struggle. To simply remember that you will never find happiness by attaining that which is outside of you will save you a world of strife. Whether you yearn for more money, more love, more status, or a better body, that want comes at the price of your happiness. Your emotional pain is often the result of your search for something you do not already have. But really, everything you need is already within you.

LIFE COACHING

When I begin life coaching with someone, almost without fail one of the first issues we explore is rooted in shame or guilt. The same happened for me when I was coached. It's uncanny. I find it comforting to know that we are not so different from each other. We all experience different versions of very similar problems. Brené Brown, PhD, a wise and prominent shame researcher, says that everyone, except sociopaths, experiences guilt and shame.

At least we're not sociopaths, right?

To free yourself from guilt and shame, you need to understand the root source of these emotions with compassion. Remember, you are so much more than your mind, body, or thoughts.

The Difference Between Shame and Guilt

Shame and guilt often feel similar, but there is one stark contrast between the two: Shame is the feeling that "I am wrong, unworthy, not enough, etc.," and guilt is the feeling that "I have *done something* wrong, unworthy, not good enough, etc." Shame is the feeling that we, ourselves, are bad in some way. Guilt is the feeling that our behavior is bad. Both emotions can be traced back to powerful belief systems and habitual patterns that must be rewritten.

No matter how deep these beliefs go, guilt and shame are just the resulting emotions of sentences we tell ourselves over and over until we believe them. When we discover where the belief comes from, we can look at it safely from different angles and with compassion. From this safe distance, we can choose to not believe the destructive thoughts anymore. Our perspective shifts.

Have you ever felt as though, no matter what you did, it was never enough to please someone important in your life? You may have felt guilty at times for not *doing* the right thing, but the real pain comes from feeling as though *you,* as you are, are not good enough. That's shame. It's tied up with who you are as a person. No matter what you do to change your situation, you still feel "less than."

Or maybe you tend to feel as though you are unimportant or invisible. You just want to be loved and to matter to the people in your life, but you continually feel let down and unseen. You may feel guilty for not doing everything you could to earn that love and a place in the spotlight of someone else's heart, but the real pain comes from feeling as though you aren't important; you aren't loved, no matter what you do. That's shame. Again, it's tied up with who you are, not what you do. We choose not to acknowledge or spotlight ourselves in our own lives, and so being the apple of someone else's eye becomes our life's mission.

You may experience one of these two scenarios, or maybe you experience both at different times. Either way, it hurts. A lot. These are patterns that begin early in life and play out again and again in different situations and relationships. We pile up different

WEEKS THREE & FOUR: THE EMOTION EXPERIENCE

behaviors (like avoidance or attack) and layers of emotions (like anger, sadness, or indifference) on top of this deep-seeded shame. But when we dig down to the root, we find a hole that never quite gets filled the way we need it to be.

With feelings like these simmering under the surface, it's no wonder that you aren't living up to your life's potential. It takes a lot of effort and energy to battle these emotions day in and day out. When you first start questioning a belief rooted in guilt or shame, your brain will bring up all sorts of evidence to prove it correct. "What have I done wrong now?" is a feeling that hints at a deeper level of guilt that wails, "I can't ever do anything right because…" Then you fill in the blank with, "I'm too stupid/ugly/lazy/etc." What started with guilt can end in shame by the formula: "What I do is never enough, and so I am never enough."

When you begin to explore negative thoughts, emotions, and behaviors in your life and from the past, remember that at the root, you only want to feel like you are enough and that you matter. When these basic needs are not met in your life, the thoughts, emotions, and behaviors that result can quickly create trouble. Unpacking those thoughts, emotions, and actions can take a lot of work.

Shame was the heavy stone that I carried around with me wherever I went. When I finally learned to roll it off my back, the lightness and love I felt was one of the most intense experiences of my life. Before I released it, I sabotaged my relationships when they started to get intimate in fear of being discovered for the worthless being I thought I was. Before we were married, I broke it off with my current husband about five times over the course of a year before I learned how to dissolve my unworthiness beliefs. When he showed up with flowers and poetry, I cursed and snarled at him like a rabid animal in pain because that belief had so much power over me. It had to be pulled up from the root for me to allow his love to truly reach me.

When I finally began making accomplishments in my life, I hurt myself with food and drugs to match and numb the pain I felt on the inside. I was unable to sit with my emotions. It was like when my light started shining too bright within, no matter how hard I worked for it, this belief would swoop in and snuff the flame, and I would spiral back into misery, self-loathing, and the heaviness of shame.

Take a few moments to write down some times in your life when you felt guilt and shame. Notice the thoughts that arise and remember that many of them are your opinions and judgments, which trigger emotions that lead to actions that yielded results.

> **One of the most powerful human experiences is to sit with your emotions, just as they are.**

When you strip everything back to the simple facts, you will see how quickly a situation can get out of control based on little more than you trying to protect yourself from feeling worthless or unimportant. You started this work over the last two weeks. For the next two weeks you'll continue, now with a focus on your emotions.

Sitting with Emotions

One of the most powerful human experiences is to sit with your emotions, just as they are. We addicts are so used to numbing our emotions, avoiding them, or covering deeper emotions

WEEKS THREE & FOUR: THE EMOTION EXPERIENCE

with anger and "toughness." To simply experience an emotion, as it is, is something we are not comfortable with.

You may think, "But that's the problem—I do experience emotions." What you are actually experiencing is your *resistance* to your emotions. It often involves anger. Let me explain.

The first time I met Frannie Hoffman, one of my spiritual teachers, she told me I needed to learn to stay connected. Just by looking into my eyes she could tell that I kept disconnecting with myself.

I didn't know what she meant, but I was upset that I kept displeasing her by doing something I wasn't even aware of. My whole body tensed from all the self-judgment. This was how I disconnected. It was like a light switch that I kept turning off. It wasn't until I took some deep conscious breaths and softened my body that I came into the present moment. I felt connected. The light came back on.

With the light on, my body relaxed and I felt vibrations. I was unfamiliar with so many sensations. I joke that the first time I really felt my emotions, it felt like an orgasm. But it makes sense—it was the first time I was able to process my emotions through the vessel of my body. The important part was being present. Feeling the effect in my body as all the resistance faded in an instant helped me to understand the power of presence. It began a conscious practice of awareness for me, and helped me develop the patience to process and be with my emotions.

Sitting with emotions—especially when they are difficult emotions—is a challenge for most people. But the only way to become comfortable with these emotions, and thereby lessen their negative impact on you, is to be present with them. It's a practice in mindfulness.

No Mud, No Lotus

When we first emerge from addiction, there is a defrosting period. We go from feeling numb to being bombarded by a tsunami of emotions, which leaves us feeling battered and bewildered. That's what it's like to get sober. These waves continue to come, and your ability to handle them will determine your outcome. You may find that you seek other substances or behaviors to numb your emotions, like caffeine, nicotine, shopping, sex, food, or exercise.

Your mind is trying to avoid deep emotions because they are uncomfortable. You might be afraid that such emotions might drive you back to your addiction. Don't believe it. I promise that, like anything in life, you will get better at navigating with practice.

When you first approach your emotions, they will sting like frostbite or like a hot flame. This is only your mind's response to discomfort. It's not real, and it won't last. It is the drama your mind wraps your emotions in. The real emotions, the deep ones anyway, will feel intense and unfamiliar. It will feel like someone dropped you naked into the forest with no map or supplies. The only way out is in.

MEDITATION

Many of my clients tell me that they are an "odd duck" or that they never really fit in. "I'm just different," they tell me. Often, their belief is rooted in a feeling that they are fundamentally

WEEKS THREE & FOUR: THE EMOTION EXPERIENCE

flawed. This belief continues to show up until they get to its root, understand it with compassion—not judgment—and prove it wrong. Until that happens, we addicts will often isolate and separate ourselves because we believe we are flawed. It's a self-fulfilling prophecy.

We hold these deep beliefs of unworthiness because we have separated ourselves from a connection to the conscious whole. But that's like being a wave who thinks its separate from the ocean—it's not possible. Even though each wave looks different than the others, it's still part of the whole ocean. You are just as connected to an ocean of consciousness. You have simply chosen to think you are separate. To access this connection, you must first connect to yourself. But unless you are taught how, you will continue to reach for that which is outside of you—something you have been doing all your life, as taught by your parents, teachers, friends, and even the media.

I was so busy suppressing my emotions with full-contact sports, pills, alcohol, binging and purging, and exercise, all to shut down what was going on inside me. Any time I slowed down, all I felt was hurt. I didn't realize it, but I felt isolated because I was disconnected to God (or consciousness, the divine, a higher power—whatever description resonates with you). I had heard that the only way to God was to go within, but I knew that any place within me was filled with pain. I didn't want to go there. It didn't feel anything like what I thought God should be. But that's because I didn't bother to try.

When I finally decided to try meditation, after much resistance, it felt like I had been backed into a corner and the only way out was to just do it. I knew there was no going back the other way.

THRIVING AFTER ADDICTION

I think this is the same point my clients are at when they come to me.

To connect with yourself, you must first get comfortable with being present with yourself. That means getting comfortable with whatever emotions arise.

Inner Journeying

One of the best ways to experience your emotions as they occur is to feel how they affect your body. By using the body as a funnel for processing emotion, you will discover signs—some of which may be very familiar to you—that can help you later recognize certain emotions, preparing you to better handle them. With practice, you will find that you can come through a difficult emotion and find peace on the other side in as little as a few minutes.

It's best to start with emotions that are less bothersome. Don't begin with your deepest pain points or you might become overwhelmed. Start with something simple. A small disappointment, like showing up late for a meeting (disappointment in yourself) or a friend cancelling weekend plans with you (disappointment in a friend), will work well.

Once you recognize a difficult emotion in yourself, if possible, find a quiet, comfortable place to sit. (I have used a bathroom stall in a moment of need, which can also work. Make do with what you've got.) Give yourself permission to fully experience all emotions that arise. Trust yourself to be able to handle them. Be open to the experience.

Begin to breathe slow and deep. Relax your jaw. Release your tongue from the roof of your mouth. Relax the sides of your

WEEKS THREE & FOUR: THE EMOTION EXPERIENCE

neck. Bring awareness to your fingertips. Press your thumbs to your index fingers and notice the small sensations that start to arise from that area. Continue to breathe deeply and notice as the sensations in your body start to speak to you.

When you feel ready, ask yourself, "How do I feel right now?" and wait for the answer that describes your emotion. Sad, frustrated, anxious, defeated—recognize what emotion comes up. Next notice where you feel the emotion within your body. Your stomach might be in knots. Your jaw may be clenched. Your throat may feel tight. Your shoulders tense. Where do you feel the emotion in your body?

Once you identify the area of your body that is holding your emotion, mentally go to that space. Continue breathing deeply and slowly. Imagine the space expanding and becoming soft. Imagine the softening expands over your entire body. Then, dive through the emotion to see what's underneath.

You will find another emotion underneath the first. Sadness, shame, jealousy, anger, loneliness, and fear are commonly hidden underneath. Repeat the exercise with this new emotion until you find a sense of peace underneath your emotions. You may eventually discover that your emotions stem from a lack of your basic need—to be enough or to matter. If you get this far, continue to breath soft and deep until the feeling takes on a lightness. Eventually, it will fade and a sense of peace will come over you, or a sense that you are "home."

Use this exercise with less intense emotions until you feel comfortable working through those that are more difficult. The more you practice, the more you will be able to recognize and handle difficult emotions when they arise. Think of your emotions as waves. This exercise helps you to see the wave approach, ride it with your body, and come out safely on the other side.

Journal about your experience here:

Access Your Inner Child

For those emotions that you already know arise on a regular basis in response to certain situations in your life, you can use an exercise similar to the last to help you understand the origin of your emotions by accessing your inner child. Before you roll your eyes, hear me out. I also thought this exercise was a little woo-woo when I first learned it. But I stayed open to the experience, and it turned out to be really insightful. I find that this exercise helps me bypass some of my logical mind's walls, which often get in the way of my progress. Try it out. You may find it helpful, too.

As a small child, you took in your parents' words and actions as though they were absolute fact. What a powerful influence they had over you! As you got older, you eventually learned that some of your parents' truths are not your own. But under the surface, some of these truths became ingrained in you, running your life like the wizard of Oz behind the curtain. This exercise will help you unearth some of your deeply ingrained beliefs so that you will understand the emotions that arise in response.

Find a comfortable, quiet place to sit, and grab a paper and pen. Write down a few circumstances in your life that trigger unpleasant emotions in you. Write down the fact (circumstance), thoughts that arise, the emotion, the action you responded with, and the consequence to the action. You'll recognize this work from weeks one and two.

WEEKS THREE & FOUR: THE EMOTION EXPERIENCE

When I first did this exercise, I wrote down, "Being around food" as my emotion-triggering circumstance (fact). Here's what it looked like:

- Circumstance: Being around food

- (Look at your) Thought: I want to eat but I don't want to gain weight

- Emotion: Anxiety

- Action: I rush through preparing and eating

- Result: Digestive upset and more anxiety

Once you lay out the entire sequence, get quiet, close your eyes, and breathe slow and deep. Focus specifically on the emotion and where in your body you feel it. I discovered that I hold my anxiety around my diaphragm. My abdomen tightens and my breath becomes shallow. Notice if your emotion has a color, shape, or texture. Is it cold? Hot? Is it heavy or light? Picture the emotion within your body clearly in your head.

For example, when I journey inward I often have a circular block around my solar plexus, which is in the abdomen above the navel. It feels hard, and the texture feels porous, almost like a thick piece of coral. It usually takes on a blue color. When I feel anxious, the emotion will usually vibrate rapidly. When I feel sadness, it will vibrate slowly.

Once you have identified your emotion's "appearance," ask it to sit in front of you. Feel as though it moves out of your body to a space just in front of you. You may feel a space open up within you as you do so. Ask the emotion why you feel anxious, sad, etc., when faced with your particular circumstance. I asked, "Why do I feel anxious around food?"

Sit quietly and focus on the space around your body. You will find that the answers come as if a child is speaking. They come from an innocent and vulnerable place. My inner child likes to be cryptic. I always laugh when I get one- or two-word answers, but I always know what they mean.

For example, if I am struggling with anxiety, I might ask her, "What is this anxiety here to teach me?"

She may answer, "Patience."

If I ask, "Patience with what?" her response might be, "Yourself."

Then, if I ask "How do I have more patience with myself?" my inner child might say, "Stay with me," or "Stop leaving."

It's a fascinating process, and admittedly, it was a little creepy in the beginning. But once I accepted that messages do not only come from our thoughts, and remembered that there is an innate wisdom the body carries, I felt more at home doing this work.

If you would like to follow along with a guided meditation, visit thrivingafteraddiction.com/thriving-after-addiction-book-program and follow weeks 3 & 4 for a yoga practice, meditation, and life coaching video to further guide you.

WEEKS FIVE & SIX: SELF-LOVE

CHAPTER FOUR

WEEKS FIVE & SIX: SELF-LOVE

Mirror
The good you find in others, is in you too.
The faults you find in others are your faults as well.
After all, to recognize something you must know it.
The possibilities you see in others, are possible for you as well.
The beauty you see around you is your beauty.
The world around you is a reflection, a mirror showing you the person you are.
To change your world, you must change yourself.
To blame and complain will only make matters worse.
Whatever you care about, is your responsibility.
What you see in others shows you yourself.
See the best in others, and you will be your best.
Give to others, and you give to yourself.
Appreciate beauty, and you will be beautiful.
Admire creativity, and you will be creative.
Love and you will be loved.
Seek to understand, and you will be understood.
Listen and your voice will be heard.
Teach, and you will learn.
Show your best face to the mirror,
And you'll be happy with the face looking back at you.

—Ken Oswald, <u>Reflections of My Heart</u>

THRIVING AFTER ADDICTION

My addiction to food and affinity for pain, drugs, alcohol, and men who gave me attention took their toll. At 19, the summer before I entered university to study English and marketing, I made a commitment to myself that I was going to transform, no excuses. But it wasn't such a healthy transformation. I starved myself and worked out for hours every day even when I was completely drained. If I "messed up" on my diet, I punished myself and purged. It was the perfect plan. I lost 25 pounds. I wore all the clothes I had longed to fit into. I was so proud. And although I felt a darkness lurking in the background, I kept it at bay with my pills and distractions.

Then weird things started happening in my body.

Crippling anxiety overcame me in the most normal of moments—during a friendly conversation with one of my classmates, for example. I would tell myself, "Just act normal and get this conversation over with." I would sweat and turn bright red, and my body would tremble. I couldn't control it and tried hard to hide it. I was so embarrassed by this new occurrence that I became more isolated to avoid it.

Then I entered university, a conservatory school where I was surrounded by ballet dancers. I marveled at how amazingly thin they were. My bulimia went from troublesome to raging. I wanted so desperately to be admired and loved like them. I shamed myself constantly with comparison. Although I tried diet after diet, I had gained 20 pounds again. I was purging up to five time a day, weighing myself before and after. If I didn't lose enough weight with each purge, I'd purge again until I was puking up bile. My throat and stomach burned.

By this time, I had stopped drinking, but I remember feeling

WEEKS FIVE & SIX: SELF-LOVE

sad. I could no longer drink myself into a numbing stupor. I think that's the first time I experienced being "dry drunk"—I actually felt all the emotions I used to numb with drinking. That's why the fleeting numbness I felt after purging was so good. It hid my reality from me.

A depression replaced my drinking habits, and I slowly eased off the pills and the binging and purging. Huge waves of emotion engulfed me. A few school friends tried to pull me out of it, but I only wanted to withdraw from everyone for a while. I would snap and lash out, so they left me to my isolation.

I was forced to either replace my usual methods of numbing out, or sit with my feelings. But true to form, I eventually found another replacement. Men fit the bill quite nicely. But unlike food that I could eat and dispose of, relationships affected my heart. The pain I was trying to avoid showed up in a new form.

***

Craig was the first person who made me feel beautiful. He was my first love. We later broke up but remained good friends. We would sit around talking philosophy and drinking herbal tea. I always saw Craig as a little boy trying desperately to be loved. We both wanted to be loved, we just didn't know how.

Like many of my friends, Craig became addicted to heroin. For seven years he struggled with his addiction until he finally got clean. But depression overcame him. Years of drug addiction affected his mental health. He hung himself when he was 23, leaving a two-year-old son behind.

Craig was not unlike every other addict I have known. He

didn't know how to love himself. Craig wanted to be free from the grips of addiction, and he did get clean. But he didn't have the tools he needed to do the work that comes afterward. More than ten of my friends died of heroin overdose when I was still in my teens. I made a promise back then that I would help people in similar situations.

That's why I wrote this book. Step one is giving up the addictive substance—food, drugs, alcohol, sex, whatever. But if you don't know how to get through the day with more than just some willpower, either the addiction will creep back in or you'll end up miserable and, possibly, suicidal like Craig.

***

Love is the most powerful vibration on the planet. When you are in a state of love, your body relaxes and heals, and you are able to let go of layers of armor and resistance that have been weighing you down. The most important love in your life comes from within—it's the love you have for yourself. When you love yourself, truly, you will be able to show up for yourself every time you falter.

> **The most important love in your life comes from within**

To make a permanent and meaningful change in your life, unconditional self-love is required. Without it, you will continue to repeat destructive patterns and fuel negative relationships that keep you in "recovery purgatory"—that place where you never quite feel you are reaching your full potential. The lack of satisfaction starts to eat away at your soul.

WEEKS FIVE & SIX: SELF-LOVE

In my own life, the pain and anger I felt was so intense that when I found peace on my yoga mat, I knew I had to explore deeper. I enrolled in yoga teacher training program because yoga was where I got the most relief from the negative thoughts that kept me thinking I wasn't good enough. I wanted more of the relief I felt on my yoga mat. But it took some work.

At first, I became so hell bent on being "the best" at yoga as a way to quiet my self-criticism. I constantly scanned the room to make sure I was the strongest, most flexible, and thinnest—and that I appeared to be the most zen, or at peace. Any moment when I failed to be this "perfect" version of myself, I felt worthless and despicable, which crushed my self-esteem and sent me on a drinking binge.

Despite appearances, at that time I had no concept of true self-love—that unconditional love and acceptance we can only feel when we shed layer upon layer of thoughts and beliefs that have held us down.

How could I love the disaster I perceived myself to be? It felt impossible. I was completely convinced that the only way I could love myself was to be someone else—that person I aspired to be but never quite attained. But no matter what I did, I could never be her. If I could only look a certain way, or if I could only achieve that one thing, or if I had enough of the right friends, then I could love myself and have the life I longed for.

This illusion kept me in a destructive cycle long after I had stepped back from binging and purging, taking pills, and abusing alcohol. I still clung to something

> **An amazing side effect of self-love is that you start to draw amazing people to you.**

THRIVING AFTER ADDICTION

outside of myself.

Even though I had wonderful things going for me at the time, I couldn't take my focus off of what was wrong with myself and my life. Eckhart Tolle says, "What we focus on expands." It sure as hell did.

Love is always a choice, even when—especially when—it doesn't seem that way.

When you deprive yourself of love in the hopes that your life will become so unbearable that it forces you to make a change, you will never get to the place you want to be. Sure, that strategy may have worked for quitting your addiction, but depriving yourself of love is not sustainable. You will always be running uphill, and your endurance will diminish. Depriving yourself of love just alienates you from it, and keeps it just out of reach.

When I first tried to love myself, it didn't work. I couldn't even go there. But what I *could* do was fully accept that I had created my own reality. I no longer pointed my finger at my mother, father, friends, or anyone else. I pointed at myself. It stings to admit that you are responsible for your own results in life. The ego doesn't like it. But when you acknowledge that you are in control of your own life, then you know you are also in control of changing it.

> **When you acknowledge that you are in control of your own life, then you know you are also in control of changing it.**

Acceptance doesn't mean that you become complacent. It means that you become aware of the tools you already have in your life, and you learn how to use them to create a permanent change. Imagine a person stuck on an island with only a hammer, throwing

WEEKS FIVE & SIX: SELF-LOVE

a tantrum about needing a Swiss army knife. All he sees is his lack of a knife. He's so attached to what he believes is the only tool that can help him that he doesn't even see the utility of his current situation.

Most of us are in a similar tantrum state, upset about what could have, should have, or would have been. We don't acknowledge the hammer within our grasp. Take a good look at your life right here and now. Pick up that fucking hammer, and know that you have everything you need to make a fantastic life. It starts with you, as you are, right now.

If you are in the pattern of rejecting yourself and finding evidence to support your unworthiness, practicing self-love will feel like you are baby-giraffing it for a while—it's going to feel awkward and unnatural to choose yourself. Choosing yourself may even feel arrogant and bring about feelings of guilt. Some of your relationship roles may change as you prioritize yourself first, which certain people in your life may not like. You may even lose friendships.

When I began putting myself first, I lost some friends. I worried about it at first, but once I opened that space in my life and new, amazing people began to enter my life, I knew that I was on the right path. It will be the same for you, too. Your vibe attracts your tribe.

An amazing side effect of self-love is that you start to draw amazing people to you. It's really quite magical. My own drastic change on the inside shifted my outside completely. Eckhart Tolle says that once we get the inside right, the outside falls into place. That couldn't be more true for me.

Once I began working on myself, I began to crave meditation. I became more calm and focused. Everything started to click. When the universe pushed me, I simply surrendered. It was at this time that I decided to open a yoga studio to try to give back all I had learned. I had dreamed of it for a while, but didn't think I had the skills, energy, or leadership ability. I knew that if I opened a yoga studio, I wouldn't be able to hide anymore. I would have to show up.

As the saying goes, "If you build it, they will come." At least, that was my experience. I have met some of the most amazing people through my studio. One of the first people I connected with was one of my greatest spiritual mentors, Frannie Hoffman. She always tells me, "My greatest wish for you is that you fully accept yourself." I get closer to that every day.

NUTRITION

In 2015, 87 percent of adults did not meet fruit and vegetable intake recommendations. That's almost everyone. Chances are, you are not eating even close to the recommended three cups of vegetables each day. Vegetables contains a rich array of vitamins, minerals, and phytonutrients that support every organ and system in the body. The Thriving After Addiction program doubles or triples the recommended daily intake so that you can supercharge your nutrition.

For the next two weeks, you'll begin to eat three cups of cooked vegetables each day. By cooking your vegetables, you'll be taking some of the burden off your digestive system, which can be sensitive to raw vegetables, especially if you do not eat them on a regular basis. Cooked vegetables are also easier to eat

WEEKS FIVE & SIX: SELF-LOVE

in large quantities. Be sure to include cruciferous vegetables like broccoli, cabbage, cauliflower, and kale, which help support liver detoxification.

Note: potatoes and corn are better thought of as starches than vegetables. Keep those off your list for the most benefit. Sweet potatoes are okay in moderation because the body handles them better than white potatoes. Your best bet is to fill your plate with a variety of vegetables. This strategy will also reduce inflammation in your body, so your body can heal right along with your mind.

YOGA ASANA

This week, you will continue to add on to your Sun Salutations. The practice will take twenty minutes. In honor of self-love, you'll add heart opening postures. By physically opening your chest, an area that may be particularly guarded for you, you'll become vulnerable—in a good way—to your feelings. After backbends, many people report feelings of exhilaration or, on the opposite end of the spectrum, feelings of deep sadness. You may feel waves of emotion during or after your yoga practices this week. Let these emotions come, and watch them go, just as you practiced sitting with your emotions last week.

If you would like to follow along with a guided meditation, visit <u>thrivingafteraddiction.com/thriving-after-addiction-book-program</u> and follow weeks 5 & 6 for a yoga practice, meditation, and life coaching video to further guide you.

THRIVING AFTER ADDICTION

YOGA PHILOSOPHY

Aparigraha

A friend of mine used to say, "The quickest way to squash happiness is to compare yourself to others." Ain't *that* the truth! When you compare yourself to others, you lose your ability to be completely yourself. You feel lack.

I see this often in yoga class. One student will look content and centered on her breath until she looks over at Holly Handstands and feels inadequate and jealous. I have been that inadequate and jealous girl, striving to be like Holly Handstands. And I have been Holly Handstands, needing to feel like I can be the best in the room. Either way, that's not yoga.

The yogic principle of *aparigraha,* or non-covetousness—not longing for that which is not already yours—can be applied when you find yourself caught up in the comparison game. To help you attain this quality, you can practice pratyahara.

Pratyahara

As a yoga teacher, I try to direct my students' attention back to their own experience. I remind them of *pratyahara,* the yogic principle of turning your attention inward. It's the best way to get out of the compare and contrast game. When you feel inadequate because you can't do a particular pose, or when you feel superior because you can, you are seeking recognition from outside yourself, which will never be enough for you. By turning your attention inward, you'll be able to detach from your expectations

WEEKS FIVE & SIX: SELF-LOVE

and those you perceive others have of you, and you can just be you. In yoga, we often fix our gaze on one point as a way to focus the mind and turn our attention inward. Practice pratyahara during your yoga practice to set yourself free from the compare and contrast game. Then take that practice off your mat when you find yourself caught in this mindset.

LIFE COACHING

For many people, especially those of us facing addiction, self-love is a foreign concept. We are drawn to alcohol, drugs, excessive food consumption, sex, and spending in part as a way to run from ourselves or to punish ourselves. Accepting yourself, let alone loving yourself, can be almost inconceivable. But before you can make any lasting change in your life—before you can truly free yourself from your addiction, you must be able to accept and love yourself, just as you are. Love creates a safe space so you can journey inside and do the deeper work necessary to live an incredible life. This is powerful work, and so worth the effort.

> Love creates a safe space so you can journey inside and do the deeper work necessary to live an incredible life.

The Path to Self-Love

The following exercises will help you to uncover self-love. You will begin in part a by exploring your love for another person in your life who is difficult to love. This process will help you to unlock your love for yourself, which you will explore in part b.

THRIVING AFTER ADDICTION

Part A

Think of someone who is challenging for you to love.
Write the reasons why you find that person hard to love.
_____
_____

What thoughts do you have about this person that prevent you from loving them?
_____
_____

What conditions have you placed on your love for them?
_____
_____

What does it feel like when you choose to not love them?
_____
_____

What would it be like to love them unconditionally?
_____
_____

What is an example of something this person does that you don't like? What would it take to love this person when they do this? What would it feel like?
_____
_____

WEEKS FIVE & SIX: SELF-LOVE

How is unconditional love different than love? How does unconditional love serve you?

_____
_____

Is there ever a time that love is not a good choice? Why or why not?

_____
_____

Part B

Why is it hard for you to love yourself?

_____
_____

What thoughts do you have about yourself that prevent you from loving yourself?

_____
_____

What conditions have you placed on your love for yourself?

_____
_____

What does it feel like when you don't love yourself?

_____
_____

THRIVING AFTER ADDICTION

What would it be like to love yourself unconditionally?
_____
_____

What is one thing you do that you don't like? What would it take to love yourself when you do this? What would it feel like?
_____
_____

How is unconditional love different than love? How does unconditional love serve you?
_____
_____

Is there ever a time when love is not a good choice? Why or why not?
_____
_____

Affirmations

If your first impression of repeating affirmations to yourself is a big eye roll, you're not alone. I also resisted affirmations at first. But daily positive affirmations can bring you into a space of self-actualization, where you're ready to make positive changes in your life. They retrain your brain to host a more positive dialogue which, in turn, creates pleasant emotions inside like happiness, gratefulness, and joy. We are able to move more gracefully and sustainably in life when these feelings fuel our actions.

WEEKS FIVE & SIX: SELF-LOVE

If you have tried daily affirmations before without success, it is likely because you hadn't uprooted your shame, guilt, and attachment issues first, which will smother positive affirmations before they have a chance to grow. You must cultivate the right emotional pH with care and attention for such beliefs to grow inside of you. That's why we did such important foundational work in weeks one through four.

This week you will begin your daily affirmation practice by writing down three things you like, love, or appreciate about yourself every day. It may be difficult at first to find three things every day, especially if your mind is trained to find the negative in yourself. If this is the case, it will take some work to change your perspective, which likely also affects your perception of the world around you. But, like the other patterns you have repeated throughout your life, you have the power to alter this one.

Patterns are a survival mechanism that help the body to conserve energy. Think about how much energy you used to focus on driving a car for the first time compared to when you drive now. You had to concentrate on the actions of your feet on the gas and brake, turn signals, proper traffic etiquette, and so forth. After a few weeks, though, it gets easier. Any new habit you develop requires extra effort. If you are used to seeing the worst in yourself, in others, and in the world around you, acknowledge that it is only a reinforced pattern that you can change with effort. You become good at what you practice. So remember that if you feel any resistance to this work initially. It'll get better.

If you find these affirmations difficult, recite the following passage to yourself, either out loud or in your head, every day:

THRIVING AFTER ADDICTION

I am human,
And in my human-ness
I am allowed to make mistakes.
Perfection is an illusion.
It steals away my truth
And makes me shrink.
When I embrace myself unconditionally,
A fantastic world opens up.
When I choose to accept and not reject,
I give others permission to do the same.
I will have the courage to be imperfect
And allow God to pulse through me.
I am not my mind, body, or thoughts.
I am the consciousness that swells below
The surface like an endless ocean of love.
I am whole. I am love. I am God.

Choosing self-love will take practice, but it will eventually become second nature. When it does, your whole perspective will shift. This is the part of the program when I see my clients glow. They come alive. Many have said that it feels like they have been the walking dead, living half a life until now.

Loving Your Reflection

The majority of women, and plenty of men, have body image issues that degrade our ability to fully love ourselves. This next exercise is an intimate one that can have a profound effect on your sense of self-love. If you find it difficult to love those parts

WEEKS FIVE & SIX: SELF-LOVE

of your body you refuse to accept, this exercise is for you.

Find a quiet room and grab a small mirror. Look into the mirror so that you can see only your face. Notice your eyes, your cheeks, your eyebrows, and your mouth. Look at your entire face. Notice the judgments that arise as though they have nothing to do with you. Notice them come and watch them go. Don't take them personally—they are the result of your past conditioning. Let these thoughts float by and breathe deeply for five minutes. These thoughts are not you. Continue to bring your awareness back to your eyes using a soft gaze.

The next day, stand fully clothed in front of a full-length mirror. Scan your body and notice what thoughts come up. Notice the judgments that arise and remember, again, that they have nothing to do with you. Watch them come and go. Breathe deeply for five minutes and continue to bring your gaze back to your eyes. Imagine yourself as a child. Find the innocence in your face.

The next day, remove your clothes but remain in your undergarments. Take more time to scan your body today. Notice what judgments arise. Notice how you feel. You may even cry or get angry. That's okay. Your judgments have nothing to do with you. Watch them float away. Look at yourself and imagine layers of armor and tension fall away. Imagine yourself vulnerable yet supported. Keep breathing. How can you love yourself in this moment? What is amazing about you? Draw your attention back to your eyes and repeat, "I love you. Forgive you. Thank you."

The next day, if you feel comfortable, remove all your clothing and stand in front of the mirror. It may take a few extra days to get comfortable with this. That's okay. Do it when you are ready. Notice what judgments and feelings come up. Imagine yourself with the same innocence of a baby or small child. Imagine that all your armor is removed. Imagine that love is passing through you and soaking into your cells. Imagine the best hug you could receive. Tell yourself again, "I love you. Forgive you. Thank you." The Earth is supporting you. You are your own creator. You can choose in this moment to love and accept yourself unconditionally.

Journal about your experience.

MEDITATION

Ultimately, self-love comes down to you feeling that you matter and that you are enough—those attachment needs we develop during childhood and that follow us throughout life. For the next two weeks, your meditation will center around your primary attachment need. If you tend to feel as though everything you do is never enough, then you will repeat, "I am enough" during your meditation. If you tend to feel as though you are unimportant, then you will repeat, "I matter" during your meditation. Sit for ten minutes every day repeating this mantra to yourself. Feel as though you are enough and as though you matter. Let the reality of your mantra firmly establish within you.

WEEKS SEVEN & EIGHT: SELF-CARE

CHAPTER FIVE

WEEKS SEVEN & EIGHT: SELF-CARE

"Watch carefully, the magic that occurs when you give a person just enough comfort to be themselves."

—*Atticus*

"Fucking stupid," I uttered on the way out of my first yoga class when I was 19. The stick-thin instructor talked way too slow and had us balancing on one leg in a dark room with our palms together. Her flowery words made me roll my eyes with distain. The slow, gentle movements made me want to claw my eyes out. My mind was like a swirling tornado. When I was asked to stand still, I felt the constant prick of my own self judgments like thorns—the discomfort made me want to lash out.

There was no greater torture than to sit with myself. It made me want to hurt someone. The concept of surrendering and "connecting with my higher power" was down right offensive, and I could feel my body getting hotter and more tense. God was such a foreign concept associated with guilt and shame in my mind. I hated God. "I'm never doing that again," I vowed.

At that time, experiencing anything beautiful was painful for me because it reminded me of how wretched I was. I couldn't handle light touch. A hug or a pat on the back from a friend made me cringe. But I welcomed violence. Punch me, and we were good friends; give me a hug, and I'd recoil. I didn't look people in the eyes unless I was being challenged. I could stare down an opponent all day, but softening and allowing vulnerability and intimacy was unbearable. After all, barreling through life had served me well. It got me through college.

After college, I began my trek across the world to Japan where I lived for one year. As an English major, I got the opportunity to teach English abroad. I was drawn to Japanese culture, but it was also a way for me to escape myself.

My father sent me a yoga DVD for Christmas after telling him I wanted an exercise video. When I opened the package, I rolled my eyes until I noticed how buff the lady looked on the cover. That was enough to pique my curiosity. One rainy day, I rolled out a mat and popped it in. I began by fast forwarding through the slow parts at the beginning, looking for the most challenge. I followed along for about a half hour, and afterward I laid down on the tatami mat in my apartment. For a moment, everything shifted. It felt like I had just pulled the blue book on the bookshelf causing a secret passage to open up. My hair stood on end and my body tingled where I usually felt tension and pain. Everything softened. I felt… happy. I felt relief. It was as though, up until that point, my life had been telling me that everything is okay but in a language I couldn't understand. I finally understood.

I sat up inquisitively. Where had this feeling been my whole life? All of my pain was washed away, and for the first time in my life, I was acceptable. I was good enough, just for an instant. I felt like I was finally home. I tried to clench down on the feeling as it slipped away, but nothing could change the fact that I had finally felt God. I had tasted just enough to know what I was missing. It was as if a warm blanket and soup had been given to me for a few seconds when all I'd known before was soaking wet

WEEKS SEVEN & EIGHT: SELF-CARE

clothes in a chilly, terrifying rainstorm.

I was hooked. I had a spark of hope that peace was possible. The seed of yoga was firmly planted that day.

It was just what I needed to believe that maybe there was more to me than my body and my mind, both of which I have been fighting my whole life. Maybe there was some untapped magic underneath, after all. Maybe what I had always been searching for was never outside of me. Maybe it was always there within me.

***

The mind and body, left unchecked, will behave like toddlers—they get into everything and sometimes hurt themselves, unintentionally. To avoid traveling down this unpredictable path, in weeks five and six you are going to focus on self-care. You will establish new routines that fill the space you have created by uprooting your emotional behaviors and thought patterns, and cultivating unconditional self-love in the weeks leading up to this one.

Only after you truly feel self-love for yourself can you be ready for self-care. Imagine that you are working with a coach or mentor who asks you to make major changes in your life. If you believe this person doesn't care about you, you won't be as likely to make the changes, will you? But if the person shows genuine love and caring for you, you will be more motivated to do the work it takes to change, right? It's the same with yourself. If you don't truly love yourself, you won't have the motivation you need to care for yourself.

Be a kind teacher to yourself so that your inner student remains open to new experiences and can learn without being afraid to make mistakes. My clients who engage in a practice of self-care that comes from a place of self-love are more willing to step outside their comfort zone and ultimately start living the life they have always dreamed of.

NUTRITION

In weeks five and six you added three cups of cooked vegetables to your daily diet. Over the next two weeks you will double that amount to six cups. That's right—you are going to eat six cups of cooked vegetables every day. You are already in the routine of adding half that amount, so now you can simply double your servings, or you can add new vegetables to your repertoire. Get creative. The more variety you introduce, the more nutrients your body will take in.

The best way to plan your meals is to include two cups of cooked vegetables with every meal. Add one cup of vegetables to your omelet in the morning and include a side of vegetables to reach two cups. At lunch, eat a bowl of vegetable soup along with a side of vegetables to pair with your main dish. At dinner, add two cups of a variety of vegetables to accompany your protein.

You can find creative ways to "sneak" your vegetables in through blending and adding them to a stew or making them into a sauce. This will help you build up a foundation of minerals in the body. Most people find that they start to have more energy once they increase their vegetable intake. If you came to this program exhausted and depleted, as most addicts in recovery are, then taking time to nourish yourself will produce fantastic results in your overall mood, outlook, and emotional resilience. It takes energy to be present, sit through emotions, and fully show up. Eating plenty of vegetables will help you stay nourished.

YOGA ASANA

This week, you will continue to add on to your yoga sequence. The practice will take thirty minutes. In honor of self-care, you'll add balancing postures, which require practice. They only get easier with practice. The same goes with taking care of yourself. It doesn't just happen because you want it to, it happens when you put in the work. For the next two weeks, you will add balancing postures on to your yoga practice as a way to show up ready to work. Over time, these postures will become easier as your body becomes stronger and your mind becomes still.

If you would like to follow along with a guided meditation, visit thrivingafteraddiction.com/thriving-after-addiction-book-program and follow weeks 7 & 8 for a yoga practice, meditation, and life coaching video to further guide you.

YOGA PHILOSOPHY

Tapas

Tapas is the yogic principle of discipline. During the next two weeks, you will be focused on cultivating healthy practices in your life that benefit your body and mind. You've already created a foundational yoga and meditation practice, which is now a regular part of your life. You've added some nutritional components that are improving your nutrient intake and digestion. This week you will round those practices out with new habits that you have been longing to include in your life. You are creating habits that become the discipline of your life. This program is not just a 12-week program to be discarded afterward. You are creating new patterns in your life. You are creating a new life! It requires some effort at first, but eventually, a healthy life becomes second nature.

Saucha

Saucha is the yogic principle of purity and cleanliness. The work you have put in so far, and that you will refine during the next two weeks, will help you purify your mind and body. You will explore areas of your life that are blocking you from becoming the healthy and whole person you desire to be, and you'll find a way to remove those obstacles so that nothing gets in the way of creating your health.

LIFE COACHING

For many people, self-care is an indulgence. You either don't have enough time, don't have enough money, or don't have the energy to engage in activities that fuel your soul. Sound about right? If so, you're wrong. You *do* have enough time, you *do* have enough money, and you *do* have enough energy. I promise.

How to Create Time

When I went through life coaching school, one day the founder

WEEKS SEVEN & EIGHT: SELF-CARE

of the program was talking about how to solve problems. She asked us what problems we have. My hand shot up, "I don't have enough time," I said, disgruntled.

She looked me straight in the eye and said, "Oh, have you been gipped? I thought everyone had 24 hours in a day. Did you only get 20?"

I sunk down in my chair with the type of discomfort that can only be had when someone calls you on your bullshit story. I was required to rephrase my problem as, "I don't prioritize what's important to me, and I don't create enough time." The encounter stung, but I'm so glad it happened. It took me from victim to an empowered state of mind. Now the ball is in my court, so I can strategize how to play the game my way.

You are likely a very busy person with a hectic life. It's easy to hide behind busyness and wear it as a badge of honor. But your over-packed life is taking its toll. If you don't create some space in your life for self-care, you will burn out (if you haven't already), disconnect, and fall back into addiction cycles as a way to self-soothe and calm your whirlwind life.

We underestimate how much love and nurturing we need to be healthy, whole adults. It requires setting aside extra time. Everything else grabs and screams for our attention, so we put ourselves on the back burner again and again, until it becomes habit to ignore our own needs. We don't usually start paying attention to ourselves until something breaks down in our lives, physically, mentally, or emotionally.

It's easy to forget that you are a spiritual being having a human experience when you're constantly running from point a to point b without a chance to breathe deep and feel joy.

To create time in your life, you need to understand where your time goes. For the next three days, check in and track your actions every 30 minutes. From the moment you wake up to the moment you go to sleep, write down everything you do and the time at which it begins. Track everything. Track the time you spend checking your email, scrolling through social media, watching television, talking on the phone, driving, going to the bathroom, eating, sleeping, daydreaming, thinking—track it all.

After three days, take a long hard look at what you spend time on. You will certainly discover areas of your life that could be better spent doing something that takes care of you. Mine your days for pockets of time that you can redirect toward self-care practices.

Slow and Steady

I have noticed that I, along with my clients, love to eagerly jump headfirst into new routines because of the promise they bring of a new life. Many times, I have tried to adopt ten new habits that completely overturn my usual routine all at once.

It never works long term.

If you take on too many changes, you will eventually overwhelm yourself with strict regimens that you have no intention of adhering to. You will quickly feel defeated and give up, which may drive you back to your old habits faster than ever. Be fair and kind. Small changes give you time to permanently integrate new habits into your life.

I intentionally designed the Thriving After Addiction program to help you develop new habits and mindsets *gradually*. Week by

WEEKS SEVEN & EIGHT: SELF-CARE

week, step by step, you are building a new life. It's the only way to experience real change. True change never occurs overnight. When adding self-care practices to your life, add one thing at a time.

You likely have a long list of healthy, relaxing, or fun habits that you would love to incorporate into your life. That's okay. There is nothing wrong with creating goals. But don't plan to start them all this week. Take it step by step.

List 10 to 15 self-care practices that you would love to be a regular part of your life. Some can be small, like pausing to take a deep breath every hour, and some can be big, like taking an annual family vacation. Don't hold back. List them all here.

1. _____

2. _____

3. _____

4. _____

5. _____

6. _____

7. _____

8. _____

THRIVING AFTER ADDICTION

9. _____

10. _____

11. _____

12. _____

13. _____

14. _____

15. _____

Now look over your list. What are the three most important practices—one easy, one more involved, and one that will feel like a big accomplishment. Circle them.

Implement It

Answer the following questions for the easy self-care practice you chose above.

Why do you want to incorporate this self-care practice?
_____
_____

How do you feel when you imagine yourself doing this consistently?

WEEKS SEVEN & EIGHT: SELF-CARE

_____
_____

When would you like to start this self-care practice, and how often do you want you do it?

_____
_____

What will need to happen for you to be able to implement it?

_____
_____

Are there any obstacles to scheduling it? What are they? List the obstacles in order of most to least likely to occur, and provide a solution for each.

Obstacle: _____

Solution: _____

Obstacle: _____

Solution: _____

Obstacle: _____

Solution: _____

After you have answered these questions, you may feel a mix

of empowerment and fear. New self-care practices are unfamiliar and can trigger fear and guilt. It's all part of the process of you falling in love with yourself, maybe for the first time ever. You have been given a brilliant gift, but it's wrapped in suffering, shame, and self-loathing. Those layers are not you. As you peel them back you will find the divine buried deep within you. You are worth all the effort you put into yourself. Don't ever forget that.

Schedule It

Open up your calendar and schedule your self-care practice. Set a reminder. Tell anyone who needs to be notified. And don't break your commitment. Treat your self-care practice the same way you would an important meeting at work or a doctor appointment. Your self-care is just as important.

Next week, choose the second self-care practice from above and answer the questions in the Implement It section above and then schedule the practice. After that, once you feel ready to incorporate a new self-care practice, follow the same procedure. Eventually, incorporating self-care will come naturally to you.

Turning Inward

If you have read this far in the chapter and you are still unsure about what self-care practices will be helpful, you probably need to turn inward for the answers. Ask yourself the following questions:

How do I feel? Use your body and mind to guide the answers. For example, when I feel anxious, I usually feel it around my diaphragm. When I tune in to myself by bringing my attention to my breath, the feeling becomes very clear.

What do I need? Sit with this question and notice what answers arise.

How can I give myself what I need? When you learn to solve your own problems rather than waiting for someone else to solve them for you, you become empowered and self-sufficient. You maintain your power and no longer have to rely on others to give you what only you can truly give to yourself.

Non-Dominant Handwriting

When you find that you still need some intuitive guidance, this exercise can help. It works best if you already have some experience listening to your intuition. You may find it useful in times when you feel stuck. Suspend your disbelief and give it a try.

Sit in a quiet area. Put a pen in your non-dominant hand (so your left hand, if you are right-handed, and vice versa). Ask yourself the questions from the Turning Inward section above. Let your hand write whatever occurs to you. Try not to think. Just write what comes. The writing may come out as though it were from a child. You may have to keep prompting for a more complete "adult" answer. Ask, "What do you mean by that?" if you need more clarity. Stay compassionate and patient. Give the child's voice a safe space to answer for you. Remain curious. You may discover something fascinating and important about yourself.

THRIVING AFTER ADDICTION

MEDITATION

According to an old Hindu legend, there was once a time when all human beings were gods, but they so abused their divinity that Brahma, the chief god, decided to take it away from them and hide it where it could never be found.

Brahma called a council of gods to help him decide where to hide the divinity.

"Let's bury it deep within the Earth," said the gods.

But Brahma answered, "No, that will not do because humans will dig into the earth and find it."

So the gods said, "Let's sink it in the deepest ocean."

Brahma replied, "No, not there, for they will learn to dive into the ocean and will find it."

Then the gods said, "Let's take it to the top of the highest mountain and hide it there."

Once again Brahma replied, "No, that will not do either because they will eventually climb every mountain and take up their divinity."

The gods gave up, "We do not know where to hide it. It seems there is no place on Earth or in the sea that human beings will not eventually reach."

Brahma thought for a long time and then said, "Here is what we will do. We will hide their divinity deep in the center of their own being, for humans will never think to look for it there."

All the gods agreed that this was the perfect hiding place, and the deed was done. Since that time, humans have been going up and down the Earth, digging, diving, climbing, and exploring—searching for something already inside themselves.

WEEKS SEVEN & EIGHT: SELF-CARE

Over the last two weeks you have been meditating on your attachment need—*I am enough*, or *I matter*. For the next two weeks, your meditation practice will be to uncover the divinity within you. Sit quietly for fifteen minutes every day.

Notice your breath. Soften your body from your jaw to your shoulders. Relax your stomach, hips, and knees, and imagine dropping from your head into the ocean of your body. Notice the current and the waves of thought and sensations that gently arise and fall away. Just observe.

When you feel settled in your body, repeat "I am not my mind. I am not my body. I am not my thoughts. I am the consciousness that swells below the surface." See if you can feel that energy of consciousness. Notice the compassion and love that comes when you reunite with your true self. Once you've tapped into this space, don't try to control it. Just relax and allow it to flow through your body. It knows what to do.

If you would like to follow along with a guided meditation, visit thrivingafteraddiction.com/thriving-after-addiction-book-program and follow weeks 7 & 8 for a yoga practice, meditation, and life coaching video to further guide you.

THRIVING AFTER ADDICTION

CHAPTER SIX

WEEKS NINE & TEN: PASSION AND BOUNDARIES

> *"every now and again,*
> *you will feel a dull ache in your soul.*
> *a gentle humming around your heart.*
> *a longing for something without a name.*
> *if i ever told you to obey anything, this would be it.*
> *listen to the call of your authentic self.*
> *that part of you that lives just outside of your own skin.*
> *let it have its way with you.*
> *i have died a hundred times trying to ignore it."*
>
> —Mia Hollow

After my experience with yoga in Japan, when I finally felt like I had found what I was looking for, I picked up a yoga book called *Light on Yoga* by the master B.K.S. Iyengar. I followed along with the sequences assigned by Mr. Iyengar, excited to have a "companion" to guide me. I felt his gentle hand on my shoulder as I practiced the poses, page by page. I began to feel whole and complete. After a few years of daily home practice, I decided I wanted to learn more. I enrolled in a yoga teacher training program and my life completely shifted.

I thought the training would be graceful. I thought it would be one wonderful experience after another leading me to a happy life. I was wrong.

THRIVING AFTER ADDICTION

The training exposed the muck, grit, and shame of my life. I cried almost every day. When my teacher placed her gentle hands on my back as I took Child's Pose during a moment of weakness, it was the first time I felt someone accept me completely, even when I was vulnerable. Despite a lifetime of practice suppressing such fickle emotions, the floodgates opened.

After that yoga practice I felt like a soggy, wrung-out rag. I felt incredibly vulnerable, like being naked in front of a thousand people with all my insecurities highlighted. And yet, there was something liberating and satisfying about showing up fully. It was like cracking open a mask worn for years and bracing for something terrible underneath only to find incredible beauty and radiance.

Yoga helped me to stop binging and purging. I could finally fill the empty hole I felt with something other than self-hatred. About halfway through each yoga practice, a stillness settled in as my darkness turned to light, and I found God. I finally felt complete. But I still had a long road ahead. I had developed food allergies, a stomach ulcer, and digestive difficulties due to many years of binging and purging. I had work to do.

***

Now that you have embraced self-love and incorporated self-care into your life, you will naturally become more steady. By steady, I mean more grounded, calmer, and more in control of your responses to the circumstances of your life. When you find steadiness, your life becomes more filled with ease. You may even find that your mood stabilizes, and you'll no longer feel like a

WEEKS NINE & TEN: PASSION AND BOUNDARIES

salmon swimming upstream. You'll stop fighting with your own mind so much.

Now it's time to funnel this freed-up energy toward your passions while at the same time setting boundaries to keep you safe and your relationships healthy. Be careful to not get overzealous with your energy. Don't take on more than you are ready for emotionally, physically, or mentally, or you'll become overwhelmed.

I see this often while teaching yoga. An ambitious student will start trying postures before she is ready, and she ends up disappointed, discouraged, or possibly injured. Even when a student is physically ready for a particular posture, she may not be mentally ready for it.

Eventually, you will become your own teacher. When you are able to tap into your own intuition, life no longer feels like hard work. It unfolds like poetry as you create the life of your dreams. Being your own teacher doesn't mean that you won't find inspiration and learning from other teachers, but you will have the ability to filter new information through your own belief systems rather than abandon your beliefs for those of someone else.

NUTRITION

For the next two weeks, you will add wheatgrass to the lemon drink you began drinking daily in weeks three and four. Packed with protein and nutrients like potassium, vitamin K, thiamin, riboflavin, niacin, vitamin B6, pantothenic acid, iron, zinc, copper, and manganese, and the antioxidants vitamin A, vitamin C, vitamin E, and selenium, wheat grass packs a lot of nutrition in a small amount of juice. You can buy wheatgrass powder or liquid juice, or you can make your own with a wheat grass juicer. Simply add an ounce to your lemon drink each day, gradually increasing to three ounces over the course of a week if you want to increase your nutrient intake.

YOGA ASANA

This week you will continue to add on to your yoga sequence. The practice will take forty-five minutes. You've worked hard to establish a strong and steady practice up until now. This week you will add some seated postures to help you turn your attention inward, remain grounded, and cultivate a sense of ease. Seated postures help to open up your back, and in some cases, open your hips. You'll be settling in to experience a new openness in your practice just as you are in your life. From steadiness, you will find ease.

If you would like to follow along with a guided meditation, visit thrivingafteraddiction.com/thriving-after-addiction-book-program and follow weeks 9 & 10 for a yoga practice, meditation, and life coaching video to further guide you.

YOGA PHILOSOPHY

Bramacharya

Bramacharya is the yogic principle of non-excess. Over the next two weeks you will pay attention to the areas of your life that require boundaries. Notice where you live in excess. Is your closet bursting full of clothing? Are you working too much? Eating

WEEKS NINE & TEN: PASSION AND BOUNDARIES

too much? Drinking too much? Consumed by social media? What areas of your life could use a little pruning?

Try to understand your behavior like a scientist trying to solve a problem. Or you could take on the role of a parent trying to understand the actions of a child using curiosity, compassion, and patience. Ask yourself these questions (be courageously honest with your answers):

What is the purpose of the excesses in your life?
___
___
___

What emotion are you seeking when you participate in creating excess?
___
___
___

How can you give yourself what you need without these excesses? For example, you could practice self-care, you could practice the Journeying technique from chapter three, or you could meditate or breathe deeply.

What thoughts would help to create your desired emotions? It doesn't have to be complicated. For example, if you need to feel comforted, you could imagine yourself wrapped in a baby blanket, staring up at loving eyes, without a care in the world. Or you could repeat your attachment need affirmation, *I am enough* or *I matter*.

THRIVING AFTER ADDICTION

LIFE COACHING

A while back, there was a big fuss about the Power Ball, our local lottery game that is shared with a number of other states. The jackpot was higher than it had been in a long time, and everyone speculated about what they would do with their winnings. Gambling is one addiction I never succumbed to, but I bought $20 worth of tickets. With the exception of a few scratch-off tickets I had purchased in the past, it was the first time I had played the lottery.

My boyfriend at the time (now my husband) and I lay in bed fantasizing about what we would do when we won. We would travel and spend more time together. I would still teach yoga, write, and do my podcasts because it all brings me joy. I would spend more time on my yoga practice and go to silent retreats. My boyfriend would give half of the money to charity. (What a guy! It's no wonder I married him.) He'd give a quarter to his family and use the rest to travel with me and our Yorkie, Cinnamon.

We both felt so amazing and woke up the next morning excited about life. In fact, that whole week I felt relaxed and satisfied, even after we learned that we hadn't won the jackpot.

We had created these feelings of abundance without having one dime more in our bank accounts. In fact, I was out 20 bucks. The power of the mind to create vibrations of happiness and joy is real. You can use this same technique to bring about positive feelings in your life, and to act from those feelings.

The week when I chose to imagine I had everything I could possibly want in my life, I never felt lack. I gave my love and time generously to people. The person I was that week was exactly

WEEKS NINE & TEN: PASSION AND BOUNDARIES

the person who I wanted to be. So I started acting that way more often. It had nothing to do with the circumstances of my life. It was my mindset that kept me uplifted.

Finding Your Passion

Start thinking about what stirs your passion. What moves you to your core? What excites you? It could be anything from a hobby or activity to a dream career or goal. What gives you butterflies in your stomach when you think about it? That's your body telling you to follow that feeling.

Write a letter to yourself from your future self—the one who has already accomplished everything you can imagine, the person who has risen above and beyond what you thought was possible. What advice does she have for you? What do you need to hear from her? Take on the persona of your amazing future self, and write yourself the letter you need to read.

If you don't feel that passionate fire burning inside you, know that it's still there. It might just be buried. If a voice in your head is telling you that this exercise is not practical, you are not alone. Your mind tells you this to keep you living a mediocre life that feels comfortable but is actually restrictive.

If this sounds like you, list at least three things that make you come alive and stir your soul. Forget that voice in your head. You have my full permission to go there. I am your fairy godmother—now go dream big. If it's dressing in drag that you want, great! If it's making ice sculptures, awesome! The world needs more passionately directed people.

THRIVING AFTER ADDICTION

1. _____

2. _____

3. _____

Which one of these activities makes you tingle the most? Set aside time each week to either do it or work toward it. No buts, just action. Put it in your calendar. It's non-negotiable.

You'll thank me later.

You may have resistance when you start a new activity because the mind likes familiarity. The same probably happened when you stopped your addictive behaviors—it probably felt like you couldn't handle it at times. But do you want to be remembered as someone who never reached for her dreams or someone who was filled with life? You are retraining yourself so that you can live the life of your dreams with more energy, vitality, and love. It's never too late to find your passion.

Setting Boundaries

For you to live a balanced, happy life, boundaries must be set between yourself and others. These boundaries will help you create more time in your life to achieve your dreams without holding resentment and while taking full accountability of your feelings and actions.

When I suggest to my clients that they set boundaries in their lives, I usually get some push back. "No, no, no," they say, listing the reasons why not, fear usually at the core. You may have the

WEEKS NINE & TEN: PASSION AND BOUNDARIES

same hesitation.

I was also afraid that if I let myself shine as bright as I could with these new tools, my friends would drop away. I thought that I would become so unrelatable that my friends would no longer want to associate with me. The pressure to fit in with the pack is a real fear engrained within us. We are meant to be connected to other human beings, and when that connection is threatened, we will self-sabotage to prevent it.

If you are constantly censoring yourself, or holding yourself back when you have a strong urge to be the person you are meant to be—whatever that means for you—your light will dim. Remember that you are never alone. You are deeply loved by your creator. Your purpose on this planet it to shine as brightly as you can. If someone drops away from your life as a result of this, they are not the person you need in your life. Do not ever sacrifice who you are for people who want you to be someone else.

I once studied in a local temple with a Buddhist nun named Gen Demo who used a great analogy. She said that we bend over backward and twist and distort ourselves for what we perceive others want us to be. Then we get so angry at this impossible rainbow we have created. Don't get angry at the rainbow—you created it. And anyway, it would be pretty silly to be angry at a rainbow. (I chuckled when I envisioned myself shaking a fist in anger at a rainbow.)

I promise that I am not here to ruin your relationships. The boundaries I suggest are simply the limits you place on your personal space. It's the line you draw between your emotional responsibility and that of another. That's all. The problems begin when you believe that by setting a boundary you are hurting

THRIVING AFTER ADDICTION

someone. This is impossible if you are setting the boundary from a place of love. If your intention is to set a boundary because you value the relationship and you want your communication and limits to be clear, then you're on the right track. If your intention for setting a boundary is as a form of punishment, then you won't be successful. Try to reframe your perspective so that you can set a healthy and respectful boundary for all involved.

No one can make you feel guilt or shame. Likewise, no one can make you feel love or joy. That's your job. Your thoughts create vibrations inside you. Changing your thoughts changes your feelings, and eliminates codependency and your need to look outside of yourself for answers. From this space, you can effectively set boundaries.

> **No one can make you feel guilt or shame. Likewise, no one can make you feel love or joy. That's your job.**

The actions of another toward you have nothing to do with you. They are an attempt by the other person to feel content in some way. It may be uncomfortable to look at it that way, but it's true. Consider the act of donating to a charity, donating an organ, or adopting a child. We give because it feels good to us. It's impossible to exclude this self-satisfaction from our acts of good. That good feeling shows us that we are in alignment with our belief system. The peace we feel brings us closer to God.

Three things must happen to set a proper boundary:

Boundaries must be set from a place of love. Any boundary set amidst emotional drama will not hold up. People will treat you the way you let them. When you set boundaries from a place of love, the boundaries are mutually beneficial. They will typically

WEEKS NINE & TEN: PASSION AND BOUNDARIES

strengthen your relationship when set with love and respect.

Example of manipulation: "I want you to stop being angry all the time or else I'll never speak to you again." Everyone has a right to their own feelings. We cannot control another's feelings.

Example of a proper boundary: "Please stop yelling at me. I prefer that we speak to each other in a respectable tone. If you choose to keep yelling at me, I am going to hang up / leave."

Boundaries must be clearly laid out and discussed. Don't assume that the other person will be able to "take a hint" when you set a new boundary. If you feel uncomfortable about addressing the situation, write it all down and get clear about what boundary you need to set before discussing it. Use the questions in the next section to guide you. Unspoken or unclear boundaries will only alienate the person you are setting the boundary with.

Example of an unclear boundary: "I expect the house to be clean when I get home." Everyone's definition of a clean house is different. Be more specific.

Example of a clear boundary: When you get home from work on Mondays, please wash the dishes and load them in the dishwasher, wipe down the counters, and sweep the kitchen floor.

Boundaries require a consequence. We adults are not so different from children. We crave structure, clear directions, and some sort of predictable outcome for our actions. A consequence needs to be set so that the other person knows the boundary is important to you. The other person may resist, especially when you enforce the consequence. It's okay. Just be sure that you always enforce the consequence. Even if the other person resists at first, they will come to rely on your boundary and will understand, over time, that it was set in order to help your relationship rather than hinder it.

Example of a consequence: "I really love talking with you, but please stop talking negatively about my ex-husband. If you bring it up again, I am going to hang up."

How to Set a Boundary

Follow the questions below to help you prepare to set a healthy boundary.

What is the boundary violation?
_____

What is the boundary you want to set?
_____

The request: If you…
_____

The consequence: Then I will…
_____

What are your fears around setting this boundary?
_____

What are the benefits of setting this boundary?
_____

How will you set this boundary?

WEEKS NINE & TEN: PASSION AND BOUNDARIES

_____

How will you ensure you honor your boundary?
_____

Establishing and Maintaining Meaningful Relationships

One of the most common challenges of thriving after recovery is establishing and maintaining meaningful relationships without booze, drugs, or your addiction of choice as a buffer. I used to drink to calm my anxiety and to feel normal interacting with my peers.

The work in this program has brought you a long way toward understanding your thoughts, emotions, and behaviors. You are ready to reach out to new people without the crutch you previously relied on.

Answer the following questions to better understand how the world perceives you and how that impacts your behavior.

Describe how the world perceives you.
_____
_____

How do you feel when you read this back to yourself?
_____
_____

How would you like the world to perceive you?
_____
_____

THRIVING AFTER ADDICTION

How can you adopt these characteristics?
_____
_____

When is a time in your life when you exhibited these characteristics?
_____
_____

Every morning, you have the chance to be the person you are meant to be. When you choose to be that person, you will find that the world loves you back.

Community interaction is a vital part of a rich and enjoyable life. The good news is that you get to select your tribe. Listen to your inner guidance, or your "gut feeling," as you take on the following challenge: Talk to five strangers every day for a week.

Start with small talk. In line at the grocery store, a lighthearted comment at the bank, passing someone on the street—you can find small moments to interact with new people almost everywhere you go. If you tend to stay home, push yourself to get out more. The energy you will get from connecting to people, even in small ways, will help to fuel you.

After a week, see how you feel. If you found this exercise to be beneficial, continue to put yourself out there in your community. You may even make some new friends. Most importantly, you'll begin to harness the passion within you and shine it out into the world. This can be powerful work.

WEEKS NINE & TEN: PASSION AND BOUNDARIES

MEDITATION

For the next two weeks, your daily meditation will be a simple deep breathing meditation. You have had a few weeks to get comfortable with meditation. Now you will meditate with only the breath as your focus. This simple meditation can be practiced anywhere, any time.

Find a comfortable seated position, either cross-legged on the floor, on a cushion, or seated in a chair with your feet on the floor. Place your hands however feels comfortable: in your lap, on your thighs, or folded together. Close your eyes. Bring your attention to your breath. Begin to deepen your breath. Gradually lengthen your exhale, and then begin to lengthen your inhale. Keep your attention on your breath. Notice how your body moves in response to your breath. When your mind wanders to another thought, notice that your attention has wandered, and then bring your attention back to your breath. Notice your inhale, notice your exhale. Continue this practice for twenty minutes every day.

If you would like to follow along with a guided meditation, visit thrivingafteraddiction.com/thriving-after-addiction-book-program and follow weeks 9 & 10 for a yoga practice, meditation, and life coaching video to further guide you.

THRIVING AFTER ADDICTION

CHAPTER SEVEN

WEEKS ELEVEN & TWELVE: SHOWING UP FOR LIFE

"It's a terrible thing, I think, in life to wait until you're ready. I have this feeling now that actually no one is ever ready to do anything. There is almost no such thing as ready. There is only now. And you may as well do it now. Generally speaking, now is as good a time as any."

—Hugh Laurie

My recovery was messy. I imagine my recovery as though I was picking up breadcrumbs, then dropping a few and retracing my steps to pick those crumbs up again, while trying to find a way to keep them in my basket. It wasn't a straight path. For a long time, I was a collector of remedies. I'd try a little bit of this and a little bit of that. It wasn't until I learned how to correctly apply those remedies that I felt whole in my recovery.

After I moved back to America, the school where I taught English was embezzling money and stopped paying their teachers. I was struggling to deal with the stress of the situation yet I was desperate to keep going. So I convinced a doctor I had ADD and was prescribed Adderall to force my body out of bed in the morning. I needed this job not just for the money. I needed it to prove I was worth something.

I was living paycheck-to-paycheck, so when they refused to pay me month after month, I blew the whistle. The next morning when the story broke, news cameras were at my home. I lost all my friends at the school, and the stress of the whole situation left me almost unable to get out of bed in the morning. I laid around for months with barely enough energy to get out of bed and shower, but I realized the universe had given me a gift. I now had a chance to heal.

After a few months I was able to collect back payment from the school, so I was able to spend my time focused on healing. I poured over nutrition books, DVDs, and programs, and started eating whole foods, using high-quality green powder supplements, doing coffee enemas, and basically nourishing myself in a way I never had before. After about three months of bed rest, I started feeling well enough to practice yoga again. I also meditated, prayed, and journaled and I continued my healing through the next year.

One day I was rear ended while driving to a local park. I began seeing a local acupuncturist twice weekly for six months to treat minor injuries from the accident. The acupuncturist taught me about energy, body work, nutrition, and even some physics. It was like going to school! Between appointments I would read the books she recommended. One day during a treatment with a still point (a device placed under the occipital groove of the head), I opened my eyes and saw waves of energy on everything. I felt so blissful and just observed the beauty. It seemed my chattering brain had shut off for a while and I could see God in everything. Tears streamed down my face as I told her, "I see you. I see the light in you."

She smiled and said, "I see the light in you too." That day I truly understood the meaning of the word *namaste*, which means "The light in me sees and honors the light in you." This experience,

WEEKS ELEVEN & TWELVE: SHOWING UP FOR LIFE

along with my yoga practice, nutritional support, and healing, ended my love affair with pills and binging and purging. I started loving myself. And I had found a deeper level of connection to God. I knew it was real down into my bones.

After a two-year period of not working, I was a different person. I switched career paths and started a company called Well-Rounded Fitness. I combined fitness with principles of traditional Chinese medicine, holistic nutrition, yoga, meditation, and body work. I loved it.

I was no longer binging and purging, but I still felt weird around food and had a poor body image. I continued to reject myself despite everything I had learned. Luckily, I could pour myself into my work.

As I continued to seek healing, I came across a podcast called Inner Effort with Alan Standish. His guest that week was Brooke Castillo, a woman who seemed to have things figured out with food and body relationships. She intrigued me.

I began to listen to Brooke's own podcast and became so smitten that I wanted to do her life coach training, but I couldn't justify the cost. The same week her program was offered, I had a client come in with terrible pain. After 20 minutes of my usually effective body work, nothing had budged in her tense body. I sat her up and started using the little bit of coaching I had learned from the podcast. I asked her if she had experienced anything traumatic in the last few years. She mentioned her husband and father had died six months apart and her son was recently put into a detox facility. I asked her how she felt about this and she started to open up with tears, anger, and sorrow. It was a really beautiful experience. I just held space for her, and afterwards when I gave her hug, I noticed that her body felt like a sigh of relief. I asked her how she felt, and she said, "My pain is gone!"

It was then that I justified the cost of the life coach training, booked my flight, and gained the skill that would fully uproot my own issues.

***

In AA, we are told that our insanity led us to drink, and I fully agree with that. The mind has a tendency to fall into patterns—some good, some not so good. Breaking those patterns that do not serve you will help you recover from your addiction. The Thriving Without Addiction program is designed to help you rewrite your patterns so that you can completely heal.

By now you may have started to feel as though you have an urge to share yourself with the world in some way. Maybe you want to share your story; maybe you want to help others; or maybe you feel a new calling in life. You may also be hesitant to put yourself out there because you feel as though you are not ready, but don't let that stop you. Choosing to be your authentic self is the greatest gift you can give to the world.

It's your choice. Do you want to feel empowered and stand in your authenticity for the rest of your life? Your first response is probably, "Of course!" But it's not that easy. We say some pretty mean shit to ourselves, as you have learned by going through this program. It takes some work to rewrite those patterns.

Now that your body and mind are coming into balance, you have a continual choice about how to show up in your life. If you want to maintain a mindset of empowerment and manifest the

WEEKS ELEVEN & TWELVE: SHOWING UP FOR LIFE

glory inside you that you know exists, you will need to pay close attention to yourself. Stay connected to your mind and body, checking in frequently.

Ask yourself, "How am I feeling right now? Is this feeling in alignment with how I *want* to feel?" If it's not, then take a moment to sit with your emotion. It's okay to feel off. It happens. The simple act of recognizing how you feel when you feel it, rather than acting out on your feelings, will help you to transform your feelings with more ease. It may not happen right away, and that's okay too. Your feelings are valid. But more importantly, your recognition of your feelings is where the work lies and how the transformation happens.

When I first began observing myself, I disconnected every ten seconds or so. I had to check in with myself frequently. The commitment to transforming my negative mindset was a huge undertaking. It was like going to work 16-hour days, seven days a week. I had been letting my mind run around aimlessly. My mind was like a child, with no routine, direction, or structure—it had been getting into mischief for most of my life.

I became aware of this stream of subconscious chatter that would constantly put me down, trigger doubt and anxiety, and get caught up in petty mind games. It was like I was back in grade school on the playground with all the mean kids taunting me and nitpicking at every little thing. To face my inner bully, I uttered the mantra, "I love myself," every time that petty, malicious chatter came up. It worked so well that it became easy for me to observe my emotions and let them pass without getting caught up in the drama that normally ensued. By rewiring your beliefs (remember, beliefs are just thoughts you choose often), you can form new pathways with loving, compassionate self-talk.

Your reality is completely, 100 percent, up to you. You get to choose what you believe. So why not believe that you are a limitless force? Go all-in. Bet all your chips on *you*, and see how your life opens up.

NUTRITION

By now in the program you are probably noticing changes in your body. If you are, that's great! You're giving your body nutrients it needs to heal. If you haven't noticed many shifts in your physical health, you may need to reassess. Hormone imbalance may be interfering with your body's ability to properly nourish cells from the food you eat. I have found that intermittent fasting, which involves daily periods of fasting, helps clients who do not respond as readily to the dietary recommendations laid out in this program.

One of the safest and most effective ways to reset the body is to fast. For almost everyone, this can be a safe and effective way to regulate your hormones, promote detoxification, and heal. Fasting is a practice that has been used for thousands of years by many different cultures for spiritual and health reasons. I have personally found success using fasting, and so have many of my clients. Be sure to consult with your doctor before attempting any long-term fasting. Fasting may be inappropriate for those underweight or with diabetes or kidney issues.

If interested in fasting, seek advice and support from a nutrition professional.

WEEKS ELEVEN & TWELVE: SHOWING UP FOR LIFE

YOGA ASANA

This week, you will add the final touches to your yoga sequence. The practice will take one hour. You will add an approachable inversion pose as well as some finishing postures that help to close the practice and turn your mind inward. This full sequence is meant to build strength and balance, bring about ease, and help you to get in tune with your body and mind. It is an essential component to the Thriving After Addiction program. Practice regularly, and let yoga be a part of your life now. Over time you will come to memorize the sequence so that you can take your practice with you wherever you go. Practice, especially, on the days when you don't want to. You'll find that on those days, if not at first, it will feel like the best practice ever.

If you would like to follow along with a guided meditation, visit thrivingafteraddiction.com/thriving-after-addiction-book-program and follow weeks 11 & 12 for a yoga practice, meditation, and life coaching video to further guide you.

YOGA PHILOSOPHY

Santosha

Santosha is the yogic principle of contentment. When you experience santosha, you are completely satisfied with what is. This whole program has brought you to this point. You have spent time noticing and uncovering your patterns, taking back your power, clarifying your needs, loving and caring for yourself, finding your passion, and establishing safe boundaries. You have set yourself up for success. And the most success you could possibly ask for is to be content—truly content—in every moment of your life. There will be ups and downs, there always are. But now you are aware of them rather than falling into your same old negative habits that pull you into a cycle that ends in destructive behaviors. You can still be content in difficult moments. The practice this week will be to continually find your santosha.

LIFE COACHING

Have you ever worked really hard at something or gone the extra mile with no acknowledgment whatsoever? Not even a pat on the back or a "Good job." It's a shitty feeling. Lack of acknowledgment can lead to anger, frustration, apathy, disconnection, and resentment. And yet, we fail to acknowledge *ourselves* every day.

We overlook our own victories and accomplishments and instead focus on how we messed up or how we could have done better, or why no one else has noticed our victories. But what you focus on expands. When you constantly critique yourself instead of giving yourself praise, or when you feel unimportant, you will find more and more to critique and less and less and to validate your worth. It's a downward spiral.

The illusion that praise and recognition only count when they come from the outside is what keeps you continually disappointed. Recognition from the outside is always fleeting. You will soon be chasing your next "fix" in the form of yet more praise, but it will never be enough. You will overwork and sacrifice your authenticity to get that next nod in your direction.

WEEKS ELEVEN & TWELVE: SHOWING UP FOR LIFE

Celebrate Yourself

What if you could fill that hole with your own self-praise? When you celebrate yourself, you will create a positive feedback loop that feels truly satisfying and inspires you to continue to do those things that light you up. It's an upward spiral, if you will. When you provide yourself positive reinforcement, you will gain the energy to keep up your good behavior.

It's important that you celebrate *all* your wins, especially the small ones. If all you seek are big wins, you will miss all the opportunities to lift yourself up along the way. To modify Gandhi's saying, be the change you want to see in *your* world. When you do, you will find that the world will change in your favor.

Write down ten things that you can celebrate about yourself or what you did today. They don't need to be epic undertakings. Afterward, read them back to yourself, and notice how you feel after each one.

1. _____

2. _____

3. _____

4. _____

5. _____

6. _____

THRIVING AFTER ADDICTION

7. _____

8. _____

9. _____

10. _____

Upper Limit Potential

In Gay Hendricks' book, *The Big Leap*, he talks about something he calls *upper limit potential*. Basically, we all subconsciously believe that we deserve a certain amount of success and happiness in life. When we start to surpass this level of success or happiness, we actually sabotage our continued success so that our reality will be aligned with our beliefs.

Crazy, right?

This can manifest in any or all areas of life—relationships, business, health, etc. I used to do this (and sometimes still do if I don't keep my eye on it) in my relationships. If I achieved a certain success in my professional life, I would start eliminating people from my life who I was convinced were out to get me or who I thought I no longer needed. I believed that I could either be loved or successful, not both. If I was in a good relationship, I failed professionally. If my business was thriving, my relationship tanked. I could never maintain a balance. My life felt like a ship that was always sinking on one end or the other.

Most of us have this upper limit potential. Do you ever worry incessantly about a made-up scenario of unlikely circumstances?

WEEKS ELEVEN & TWELVE: SHOWING UP FOR LIFE

Do you catastrophize (imagine the worst possible outcomes)? If you do this, and especially if you do it when your life seems to be going smoothly, you have an upper limit potential problem.

The following questions will help you to transform your mindset about your upper limit potential.

What are you worried about that is causing your self-sabotage?
_____
_____

How do you feel when you believe this to be possible? What thoughts arise?
_____
_____

How do these feelings and thoughts prevent you from taking action in your life?
_____
_____

What do you gain from indulging in these thoughts and emotions?
_____
_____

How would you like to feel?
_____
_____

THRIVING AFTER ADDICTION

What thoughts and beliefs will help you to feel that way? (Hint: Create a mantra, or saying, that you can repeat to help you change your mindset.)

_____
_____

If you felt the way you desire, how would your life be different?

_____
_____

    Repeat your mantra often. Write it on a sticky note and tape it to your mirror. Repeat it until it becomes a subconscious belief. Think of how big companies get into our heads with their logos and slogans everywhere. You can do that same thing by consciously choosing what you want to believe and surrounding yourself with that message. When you consciously replace your original worry, you will prevent your mind from defaulting to its usual pattern of self-sabotage. Instead, you will reinforce a powerful and positive new belief. Eventually, your brain will adopt your mantra as truth, and you will embody it.

    A few examples of mantras I have used on myself and with clients:

- I am an amazing and brilliant light, and I deserve all good things.

- I support and accept myself no matter what.

- I can do this, and I *will* do this.

WEEKS ELEVEN & TWELVE: SHOWING UP FOR LIFE

- I am focused, energized, and unstoppable.

- I love every part of me.

- I am loved deeply by my creator.

- My body is healthy and happy.

- My goals are rushing toward me.

- I am open and free.

- I choose to stand strong in my authenticity.

- There's nothing to defend. Everything is an opinion.

- Love starts with me.

- I am enough.

- I matter.

If it feels better to begin your mantra with "Maybe… ," "Just for today… ," or "In this moment I can… ," feel free to soften it. Your body is your true guide. If you say the phrase and you feel a tightening somewhere or your mind begins to chatter negatively, it's a sign that your mind isn't buying what you're selling. Use a modifier and repeat your mantra often. You will find that you won't need it for long.

Goals and Priorities

In the previous chapter, you identified what makes you come alive and fills you with fire and passion. Now we are going to work those passions into your life. It's time to match the priorities you have in your head with what actually happens in your life. Remember, if you hear yourself say, "I don't have enough time," rephrase it as the more empowering, "I have enough time, I just choose to not prioritize this." This tweak can change your relationship with time and with your priorities.

In chapter six you identified three goals that you want to prioritize. List them again here:

1. _____

2. _____

3. _____

For each of these goals, answer the following questions:

Why do you want to achieve these goals?
_____
_____

How do you feel when you imagine yourself realizing this goal?
_____
_____

WEEKS ELEVEN & TWELVE: SHOWING UP FOR LIFE

How will you need to change to be the person who has realized this goal?

_____
_____

With this new information in mind, list your top five priorities:

1. _____

2. _____

3. _____

4. _____

5. _____

Are you currently living in line with these priorities?

Think about how you spent your day yesterday. Is it in line with your priorities? If not, what can you do to change that?

_____
_____

The path to realizing your goals is not always straight. There will be loops and detours. Be sure to not put your happiness on hold while working toward your goals. "Progress, not perfection," as my friend Alen used to say. Enjoy the journey.

THRIVING AFTER ADDICTION

MEDITATION

You have tried out a few different meditations throughout this program. Now it's time to settle into one that you feel most comfortable with. Which meditation feels best to you? Spend the next two weeks deepening your experience with this meditation. If you are not sure which one you like best, revisit a couple of them to determine which one you'd like to stick with for a longer period of time.

The more time you spend meditating consistently, the more benefit you will gain. Some days will feel like a total waste, but they are not. It's all part of the process. The more you meditate the more you create space between impulses and reactions. Keep with it. Over time, you will begin to see how the practice changes you. People with long-term meditation practices will tell you it's one of the most important parts of their life. You've already developed a good habit. Now keep it up. The hardest part is already behind you.

CONCLUSION

These pages can only hold so much of my ever-unfolding journey. Through the process of writing and editing this book, I have sat with and held space for the deepest part of myself as I attempt to express her through writing. Every time I sat down to write or edit, it was like open heart survey, as my friend Lady Gaga would say. During the process, I even became aware that I have a more subtle form of eating disorder called orthorexia, which I was able to shed from the time I started writing to now.

It's been quite a journey.

All of this is a practice. Yoga, meditation, mindful coaching, and nourishing the body are all radical acts of self-care. We learn to invest, trust, and respect ourselves even when the world is swirling with chaos (or so it seems) around us.

As a result of this self-care, I was able to reestablish a relationship with my eldest brother, who you read about in the beginning chapters. Initially, interacting with him brought up hidden post-traumatic stress from past abuse. But I was able to, with compassion and patience, hold space for these feelings and process them, just like I teach you in this book. Now, I can be there for my brother in a healthy and loving way, and I can truly see him as he goes through his journey of shedding addiction and becoming self-actualized.

It's a gift I didn't know would mean so much.

The following passage is from my public social media page. I try to be as authentic as I can in all arenas of my life, so I share the dark along with the light. I received a surprise call from my brother one day that inspired the post.

"He read the book I sent him, *The Yamas and Niyamas* by Deborah Adele. He liked it. He wants to start practicing yoga, but he doesn't know the poses. I plan on sending another book to show him how.

I'm detached, but in that moment I told him I was happy for him and only he could take this journey. I didn't put any chips on the table.

Whether he decides to show up or not, I hold space. I have no shame about it. They're his lessons. This is the kind of learner he is. I know that my feelings about this have nothing to do with him, and that's empowering. I take full responsibility for managing my mind and emotions during this process. These are my lessons, and I feel content knowing that."

A few weeks later I posted:

"I just got off the phone with my brother. He's in rehab and I see a shift in him. We talk spiritually. He is always very grateful. And he has started studying his thoughts. He is starting to understand why he reacts the way he does. He is starting to feel some space between his thoughts and his emotions. He pauses. He thinks about the future impact and how he will feel. He isn't so angry anymore. He feels more vulnerable and so… grateful.

Unless we understand ourselves and start loving ourselves, we cannot change. But that change is possible with radical acceptance, support, and an open mind. The man I once hated for beating on me is now one of my favorite people to talk to. Imagine that."

I typed out that last post just as I was thinking about how to end my book. Telling this story here seemed just right. Thanks for joining my on this journey. I hope to be with you, in some small

CONCLUSION

way via the pages of this book, as you travel your own journey of healing.

THRIVING AFTER ADDICTION

ABOUT THE AUTHOR

Erin Colleen Geraghty is an addiction and eating disorder recoveree. She struggled with drinking, pills, and bulimia for 12 years. After a divorce, getting laid off from work, and being completely adrenal fatigued and bed ridden, she healed herself through nourishing her body, yoga, meditation, and life coaching.

She now owns a yoga studio called Thrive Yoga & Fitness, a spa establishment of collective healers called Thrive Yoga Therapies, a Recovery Coaching Company and podcast called *Thriving After Addiction*, multiple meditations on Insight Timer, and for fun plays Roller Derby as Yakuza Girl with the Bradentucky Bombers Roller Derby League. She is happily married to her husband Brendan Linzi with their Yorkie pup Cinnamon in Bradenton, Florida. She is a yoga therapist and a recovery coach that does in house and long distance sessions.

Made in the USA
Columbia, SC
11 December 2018